Essentially Mira

Essentially Mira

THE EXTRAORDINARY JOURNEY BEHIND
FOREST ESSENTIALS

MIRA KULKARNI

HarperCollins *Publishers* India

First published in India by HarperCollins *Publishers* 2022
4th Floor, Tower A, Building No. 10, Phase II, DLF Cyber City,
Gurugram, Haryana – 122002
www.harpercollins.co.in

2 4 6 8 10 9 7 5 3 1

P-ISBN: 978-93-5489-527-2
E-ISBN: 978-93-5489-557-9

Typeset in 11.5/15.5 Adobe Caslon Pro
Manipal Technologies Limited, Manipal

Printed and bound at
Thomson Press (India) Ltd

For Papa
Knowing you are still there
as always

Contents

1

A Different View

It was the same familiar spot at the far end of the playing field.
I stared at the valley view ahead of me—a pine forest, with the same white mountains rising in the distance against the same vast billowing sky. Nothing had changed since we came here four years ago. But at this moment my thoughts were pinning themselves to a future they couldn't see.

'What will my life be like? Who will I be? Where will I be?'

There were no answers. The wind was sharp through the pine air.

My mind was cold and filled with questions. It stared at the forests as if looking there for answers.

My long unruly hair rose heavily in the cold wind, restrained in a rubber band. Out of the cream flannel collar came a face with eyes the shade of burnt hazel.

I was fourteen. There was no answer.

Tara Hall was the same as it had been when I was first brought there. Each year going by begging Papa not to be sent back to boarding school. And it was the same now.

My favourite place was here, where I was standing, at the end of the playing field.

An iron mesh was in front of me, protecting the school from the valley tumbling down below.

I liked its desolation.

It would take time before the teachers would find me there and force me to come back to the games that were of no interest to me— badminton, basketball, tennis. They were wonderful games; I had no problem with them. But I just wasn't the type that played sports.

I liked reading, curled up quietly, away from the crowd.

I was best left alone. Had somebody asked me what my hobbies were, I would have given it some thought and come out with the same two: reading and imagining vivid, clear, sharp pictures in technicolour.

And now I was imagining.

Struggling to come up with a future. What would I be doing, say, ten years from today? It was a very real question. It was worrying to me because there was no image this time. There was not even a *clue*. Would I be a wife? Would I find myself in a job? Would I have children? Or would I be a nun? The Irish nuns who ran Tara Hall possibly led safe and comfortable lives.

I shuddered without knowing why. And then I thought of film stars. There was a girl in school who was related to a film star, who was always asked questions on how film stars live. Would I be a film star? Or a model?

There were no answers at all as I stood there—in my grey woollen skirt and knee-length socks, huddled in my flannel blazer, always freezing, always wanting home-made food, resisting the endless games, in that elite Shimla boarding school that I could find no complaint against, except that it was not home.

———

I think we were in class five or six when my friend Sonu, who was with me in class, used to come down to Delhi just before school reopened, and we used to drive up to Shimla together in the car. Her name was Anita Malkani and she lived with her parents in one of the nicer buildings in South Bombay, with lovely views. The countdown would start with Sonu's arrival. She would always bring boxes of Bhel Puri packed by her mother, which we all looked forward to devouring.

Nights were invariably spent with Biji, my grandmother, with Sonu and me on either side, listening with rapt attention to her beautifully embellished stories about the Sikh Gurus. 'When Guru Gobind Singh came in riding on a white horse'; 'When the Guru's children were buried alive within a brick wall'—everything seemed larger than life when we were with her, and we would fall asleep thinking of brave knights in shining armour.

2

Home

We lived in a house, which was like many old homes in Delhi at the time—somewhat colonial. Spacious verandas interspersed with pillars. The rooms were large, with high ceilings and huge expanses of garden. It was in a wide lane with enormous gulmohar trees on either side, which were a stunning riot of flames when they flowered. There was a large swing hung between two trees in the centre of the lawns, masses of flowers in neat terracotta pots that bloomed seasonally and rows of impossibly perfect vegetables in a garden on the side.

There was a beautiful grapefruit tree with glossy leaves. The fruit had a bright pink centre when it was cut, which we often had for breakfast with brown sugar and a shaving of ginger. There were also two mango trees in one corner, which were my favourites. Slices of raw mango with chilli-flecked salt were slices of heaven.

My younger sister, Anuradha or Choti as she was called, was very fond of animals, so my father had made a menagerie for her, which was on the right, behind the house. It had wire-netted partitions with various animals at different phases of our childhood, ranging from deer to rabbits to white mice. I particularly hated the white mice. It used to be Choti's favourite pastime when she was annoyed to bring one out and slip it into my dress. She would invariably find me screaming with horror and running off, and she would squeal in delight!

One of the many vivid memories about my childhood was that my mother used to dress us both in matching outfits, which was fine when I was younger, but I found it increasingly irritating when growing up. 'Mummy, please, I can't wear the same clothes as her all the time! It's too babyish!'

'Oh, come on, beta, it looks so cute.'

It wasn't, of course, but Choti wanted to do exactly what her sister did. She wanted to wear the same clothes as me, eat only what I ate and play only what I played. Once, I remember at a birthday party, I put something on my plate which I really disliked and pretended to eat it and, true to form, she did the same. She looked up after she bit into it, realized that I actually hadn't eaten it and came to pummel me with her small, clenched fists. 'Remember the mouse?' I said in triumph.

We used to walk down from Southend Lane to Khan Market to a lending library, which had loads and loads of dog-eared books on everything. You could borrow three books at a time, which never lasted me for too long, so the visits were frequent. I used to devour books. They could have been anything. Enid Blyton, then Georgette Heyer, Agatha Christie and later the delights of P.G. Wodehouse and the suspense of Edgar Allan Poe. We had to have the lights out at eight p.m., but I would often be caught reading under my quilt with a flashlight, leading to serious consequences, including stopping my ration of Coca-Cola!

Home was not home without the mention of Prem Singh, who was our Major-domo. He ran our household with perfect rhythm, whether it was our parents' dinner parties, or our lunches with shepherd's pie when the potato crust was made to look like a bird in flight (that was when he thought we deserved a treat!). He was such an integral part of my childhood, listening patiently to our growing-up concerns and saving us from our mother's wrath, while showering us with unconditional love. He could not come with us to Madras when we had to relocate, as his entire family was in Tehri Garhwal, and going to the South was like crossing the seven seas for him. It was a painful and tearful separation on both sides, and the first instance of many that would come later.

3

Boarding School Holidays

School holidays! Biji, friends, my cousins Nisha and Vikram, Prem Singh's food, books, the garden and precious privacy.

The bathroom … oh, I loved my bathroom—large, clean, fragrant and without a stopwatch keeping the time. And I loved the drawing room too—with sofas along the wall, curved ones that created so much space to sit in a party.

Then came the best part of the room, where my parents had the music and the bar. The bottles had different labels on them and were in different shapes. Together with the diffused lighting, they looked like an orchestra ready to tune you into that celebratory mood. The bar would light up separately with the press of a switch. Then the different kinds of glasses would come into view—tall ones, beer mugs, flutes for champagne, round ones with stems for wine, big-bellied brandy ones and tiny ones for liqueurs. They glinted under the light of the bulbs, promising magic.

We kids would wander through this adult realm, admiring the soulful women and slick men on LP covers and letting our legs dangle as we propped ourselves on the bar stools.

Mummy and Papa were often out for dinner.

———

The house was quiet. Biji was busy in her room doing her evening Paath, the Sikh prayer.

Nisha and Vicky looked bored. We walked aimlessly along the empty drawing-room sofas. A small table lamp brought a dull glow into the darkness of the room. Then we reached our favourite piece of furniture: the bar. I got an idea.

'Let's play Bar-Bar.'

'What's that?' The other three asked hopefully.

'One person makes the drinks and serves them. And the others are the party guests, holding the drinks in their hands and chatting.'

Nisha, Vicky and Choti looked at each other and nodded their heads vigorously. 'Yes! Yes! Yes!'

'Who'll serve the drinks?' Nisha asked.

'I will?' Vicky said, looking hopeful.

'I will,' I said. I went and commanded Prem Singh to give us four bottles of Coca-Cola. He said no, as our Cokes were rationed. I explained that we had to play Bar-Bar.

Muttering under his breath, he relented after some time. I came back with the four bottles of Coke. We switched on the bar lights. We pulled off the cloth dust cover of the record player. We turned the switch on the wall and got out one of Papa's long-playing records. I was over eleven now. This was not too hard for me. Bar-Bar had begun.

All the excitement and pleasure of a party came alive for us. We acted relaxed over our tall cool Cokes in long glasses and hung about the bar or chatted on the sofas as we took occasional and small sips, as though they were whisky or rum. We threw our heads back and flung an arm on the back of the sofa or crossed our legs as we sat, just like the adults would have done. We put on our long plastic necklaces and wore Mummy's sandals. Vicky changed into his 'going-out' slippers—he didn't dare wear something of Papa's.

After the Cokes were over, Bar-Bar had worked enough magic. And anyway, we were being bundled off to dinner and bed. We had happy, satisfied smiles. It became a ritual that winter.

After a few Bar-Bar evenings, which happened whenever my parents would go out, I was pouring the Cokes—one bottle each into one tall glass—for the three 'guests' when I was struck by a genius idea.

It was so obviously clever. I was awestruck by its simplicity.

I announced to the company of little people scattered around the bar, 'Today I will serve a new drink.'

Nisha, Vikram and Choti were surprised. 'What new drink?'

'One peg of Coke topped with milk till the rim of your glass. Here's the milk.' I had pulled the milk jug out of the fridge and put it on the bar tabletop. The 'guests' looked kind of uncertain and one or two screwed up their noses, confused about why this was exciting. But I told them why: 'It's the latest in America!'

Everything from America was beyond reproach. So, this cleared all doubt. 'Wow!' They were really excited.

'Cheers!' we all said. We sipped the milky drink slowly (and fashionably) as before, till it finished and the game ended.

The part that was off the official Bar-Bar script was the clever stroke of genius in my eleven-year-old mind: I would quietly drink all the Coke left in each of the four bottles!

Years later my cousins would laugh about this: 'Miru, that drink was awful but since you said it was American, we were over the moon. And what torture! Remember the weird taste till today!'

Those were fun times. But underneath lay troubled waters.

4

Madras

When I was almost sixteen and Choti barely twelve, my father was transferred to Madras. It seemed to be a different land at that time to anyone living in the North. The new house was in the process of getting ready, so we were to stay in a hotel till then.

We moved and found ourselves safely deposited in a comfortable cottage at the Ashoka Hotel.

The Ashoka Hotel was supposed to be the most superior of the hotels that Madras had at the time. The hotel was conceived as a set of cottages, set at comfortable distances from each other.

It was from The Ashoka that Choti and I would go to our new school, the Holy Angels Higher Secondary School.

Every day we would pass a cottage or two on our way out from the hotel and then we would come into this new country, Madras.

New rules came into my teenage horizon. New codes of dressing. How did women dress here? Their hair was always oiled, except when they washed it. Was that why it was so thick, so long? On the oiled buns and plaits, however, you could be sure of seeing a braid of fresh, fragrant flowers to adorn them. They often had bare feet when they walked and their saris stopped above their ankles.

But the saris were beautiful silk ones, traditional to the area. Here, women wore solitaires in their ears and diamonds in their nose pins. Men wore caste marks on their foreheads. Everyone did their puja very early in the morning and bathed before the rest of the day followed. By the time we were on our way to school, Madras, I reckoned, had already crossed through its morning. Families had effortlessly woken up at dawn and performed their daily religious rituals. A far cry from our breakfasts, which we ate half-awake.

In Madras, it was always warm and humid. There were no summers and winters. The same set of clothes worked the whole year round! Coming to the Madras roads, for the first time in my life I saw cut-outs—towering, technicolour, larger than life—along all the roads, of M.G. Ramachandran, the then Chief Minister of Tamil Nadu, and J. Jayalalithaa, the reigning film star, amongst many other swashbuckling heroes and buxom heroines.

Even God was not given such a status wherever I had lived before this.

I was like a sixteen-year-old sponge for such things, noticing these details more than ever.

We stayed at The Ashoka for about three months. Papa came and went to and from Delhi.

In one of the cottages that we would pass on our way to school lived a young man. He was introduced to us by a friend of my parents who had some connection with films. Madras was the film-industry hub in those days and he became friendly, on neighbourly terms with my mother.

One day, he met us in front of our cottage and asked my mother, 'Do you all want to see a film shooting?'

We had never seen anyone shoot. For that matter, we had not seen anyone from the movies before. When I heard him talk to my mother, I became curious.

'A film shooting? How come you are connected with a shooting?' Mummy asked.

'Well, I want to be an actor. I am trying out a career in acting.' His smile was shy and polite all in one, if that's possible.

Oh, I thought, an actor! That's how actors look? He looked just like us.

He could have been anyone—a cousin or one of the children of my parents' friends who would come over. A regular guy, maybe a little taller?

He said, 'It's in a movie studio called Vijaya Vauhini Studios.'

We had heard this name somewhere. He was hesitating a little as he spoke. 'Yes, yes!' we said. 'That's kind of exciting.'

We went to watch the shooting. We couldn't wait to see how it would be. We reached Vijaya Vauhini Studios. Soon, we were on the set, since he had left word at the gates. That day there was something like a bus on the set. And there he was! Our neighbour was on that bus-like thing.

We were thrilled. There were one or two other people with him on it too. Holding my breath, I waited, feeling a bit tingly watching a real film shooting live. The shooting began. There were all kinds of people outside the bus doing different jobs. How many people and how much work, I thought. Then water was poured over the bus to make it look like rain. Again and again. They kept throwing water. After a while I realized this was all that was happening. Retakes and retakes of a bus in the rain with three people inside it. It was beginning to get boring. Soon, we were fed up. It was not so exciting any more, but yes, we did get to see a real shooting.

Our neighbour realized at some point that it must be getting monotonous. He came up and asked if we would like a Coke or something. Of course we would! Mummy protested but he said, 'No, please, do allow them!'

Finally, we came back home, a little earlier than we had planned.

A couple of weeks later, I was going to school when a golden-coloured, fancy-looking car slowed down next to me. It was our neighbour.

'Hi!' he said.

'Hi! Nice car. New?'

'It's my first imported car!' he said. He looked very happy. 'Do you want to come for a drive? Just a quick round?'

'I would like that,' I said quickly, making sure my mother had not seen us.

He stretched across and opened the passenger door for me to get in.

We went—where else but to Marina Beach. It was a short drive around the beach. It would have been over in ten minutes.

Then he said, 'Would you like to have an ice cream? To celebrate?'

I nodded. I really felt pleased for him. Wow. He looked so young … and to own that big car!

We ate the ice cream and drank coconut water as he had spotted a coconut seller right next to the ice-cream van.

'What do you think?' He was really upbeat about his new car.

'It's fab!'

'I know! Have to tell my mother straight after this.' He smiled. 'She doesn't even know yet.'

His eyes looked away, probably thinking of her reaction when she would see his car. Then we drove back.

We returned to the hotel. I sat with him for a while on the steps of his cottage. He chatted about how he had given up a job because he really wanted to act. Finally, I thought it was time to leave. As I began to get up, he reached out, ruffled my hair and said, 'Study hard and do well.'

Soon after that we moved to our own house. We never met the actor again.

Years later, I would still replay those memories with amusement because that man in the cottage next door was none other than Amitabh Bachchan, the future superstar of Bollywood.

Strangely, I never met him again.

I'm sure buying his first car is a time that he will not have forgotten.

———

Our house in Madras was on Spur Tank Road. It was a beautiful house, almost like a movie set by itself. It had all the classic mansion cliches that one would see in movies—a fountain in the centre on the ground floor, a staircase grandly spiralling up on both sides, the drawing room fashionably sunken.

The bedrooms were upstairs with balconies overlooking the front garden. The look of it reminded me of Emily Brontë's *Wuthering Heights*.

My Bharatanatyam classes would take place at home. I remember reluctantly waiting for the teacher, who would arrive punctually in his veshti and lungi, each time dashing my hope that he would be unable to come for once. So, I learnt Bharatanatyam in spite of myself.

Biji kept up her routine of staying with us for parts of the year even in Madras. She was still beautiful. She was tall and very fair. Her salt-and-pepper hair would be in a jooda. She was fanatic about cleanliness—hands had to be washed every time when you came into the house and shoes dusted properly after a walk.

I was at that keel-over stage where suddenly, from a girl who looks more and more like a woman, you cross over and finally more or less become one. Evidently, I had not keeled over enough just yet. All my Mills and Boons were awash in heartbreaks and perfect loves, both in the same story. And my heart was duly ready to break—just so ready.

'What are you reading?'

'Nothing, Papa. A novel from the library.'

I used to cover the Mills and Boons in brown paper to prevent his eyes from landing on the taciturn men and desirable blondes on the dog-eared covers.

How perfect were those loves … just the way I would want them—but not for Papa. He, it seemed to me, definitely belonged to Victorian times.

I was sixteen and in class ten—a school senior. But there was no question of access to any boys.

There I was, in a house like a movie set, studying in an all-girls' school. Make-up was a no-no, miniskirts were banned and phone calls from boys were not allowed.

Where was anyone going to sweep me off my feet like they did in my books and in my fantasies?

That was when, one mundane evening, Lalit Badhwar walked into our house.

Lalit had come to see Papa. I was pottering about downstairs, still in my school uniform, when he walked in to see my father for the Doon School reunion. Papa was part of the committee for the Doon School Old Boys' Reunion and Lalit was a Doon School boy.

Lalit was with another former schoolboy like himself.

He and his friend, Mike Dalvi, were both handsome, in their twenties and newly finding their feet in their jobs in Madras. Mike was already something of a legend. He had been the Head Boy at Doon and Cricket Captain at St Stephen's and many girls, I was told, were swooning over him! I suddenly became conscious of my clothes. There was an ice-cream stain on my school shirt. And why hadn't I changed out of my uniform? Now they would know that I was in school.

They smiled at me. How handsome! My breath caught itself midway and then, weirdly enough, I was suddenly aware of everything around me—the fountain outside, the beige of our curtains, the shine of the banisters of the staircase, the faint male smell of their colognes combined.

'Hi,' I heard one Greek God say. 'I'm Lalit. Lalit Badhwar.'

I looked away. I wanted to look like nothing had happened. So, I looked at his friend Mike instead.

'Is Chander in?' He was continuing to speak! 'We had fixed to meet him at six this evening.'

'Uhh ... uhh okay ...'

I caught the expression on their faces. They had amused smiles.

Even in that innocence of sixteen years, I could tell that they knew the effect they had on women. Before this could register, the study door opened. Papa's head popped out. He said, 'Oh good. You guys are here. Come in.'

I ran up to my room. I felt out of breath.

My heart was beating against the ice-cream stain. I sat on my bed. The cool bedcover touched my calves as my feet dangled.

I stared out of the window and aimlessly watched the tops of trees stabbing upwards into view. There were clouds gathering before the rains and thunder seemed to be drumming in my ears.

After that encounter, life developed a momentum of its own. Fluffy cotton-candy days passed by, one after the other. Everything became clear. Life parted into two halves—into what was necessary for a chance to meet Lalit and what was not.

The Madras Gymkhana Club became ground zero because I had found out that Lalit often went there. We used to go there too, to swim on weekends or sometimes even on weekdays to have sandwiches and chips or a Coke. Common ground.

So now I would find out what days Lalit was going to be in the club and manipulate my schedule, the car, the driver and, of course, Papa, to make sure I casually went there at the same time.

Should I wear the jeans or the white slacks? Maybe a ponytail in a rubber band?

Finally, at the club, Lalit would arrive and I would languidly say 'Hi' and pass him by as he said 'Hi' back to me.

Smooth and casual. That's all it was. Just three delirious seconds each time.

Many months passed. Then one day something new happened. I wished him as usual at the Gymkhana Club.

'Hi,' Lalit said.

As I turned to move on as usual, I heard his voice say another sentence.

'Mira, would you like to come out for dinner with me and my flatmate?'

I couldn't speak. Then I stuttered, 'Yes! Yes. Would like that.'

Madras was sweltering as the lawn sweated under the sprinklers.

'Good, then. Be ready. We can go early to the Chinese restaurant near your house.'

My mind raced on how to do this. *Papa!* Then I remembered that Papa was away.

I would just have to ask Mummy. I begged her to say yes and promised I would come home at whatever time she said.

The day of the dinner was finally upon us. I was drained with all the hours that had passed since the moment I had been invited.

I had still not decided on the finally final thing to wear. My room had been filled with rejected clothes and cleared by the maid two days in a row.

As the evening approached, I went to my mother.

'Mummy, please let me wear a sari of yours?'

'You don't know how to wear it,' she said. 'How will you manage?'

'I will manage if you lend me your high heels.' I was going to make this happen. I had to look older. I could not wait to be twenty.

Mummy gave me a queer look, a mixture of curiosity and amusement. 'Hmm ... okay,' she said.

I practised and practised walking in the heels. I had mastered it in a few hours that just flew by.

But new hurdles were rising relentlessly. No blouse! We needed a blouse too. I dived into her cupboard for her blouse.

I pinned the blouse on the sides. The large garment made my body feel slim and willowy.

Then I went to Mummy's dressing table. I was hobbling as I balanced my sari, the heels and the pinned blouse, and I reached out for her lipstick.

After I had put on lipstick (I think it was a not-so-suitable colour), Mummy raised her eyebrows and said, 'Is that my blouse? Hmm … and my lipstick?'

I nodded.

'Not bad,' she said.

The clock on the wall said 7.30 p.m. The staircase spiralled grandly down into the lobby outside our drawing room.

As the clock let out a single gong, I heard the front door being opened by Mutthaiah, our bearer.

'Coming,' I said in a voice cool as a cucumber, as though I climbed down the stairs in a sari and high heels every day.

I walked to the top of the stairs from my bedroom, feeling as twenty-year-old as I would have wanted. Pleased by all the confidence that my practising had given me, I began to descend the stairs. Now, however, the sari was bunching up as I stepped onto the next step and then the next.

Suddenly my heel caught on the edge of the sari and I tripped. In horror-filled slow motion, I felt myself begin to fall. Then I rolled all the way down to the bottom of the stairs.

My hair, my petticoat, my sari were all flying awry as I landed with a dull thud ten steps away from the boys. There was a collective male gasp. My head spun. My knees were hurting. I wanted to kill myself. As Lalit and his friend rushed to help me up, Lalit said, 'Are you okay? By the way, this is Bunty.'

Bunty looked sorry for me.

'I'm fine,' I said.

'Sure you're up for dinner?'

'Yes, of course!' I said, as though people fall every day. My sari was beginning to slip off.

I grabbed a bunch of pleats and deftly shoved them back into the waist of my petticoat.

At the Chinese restaurant they ordered a beer.

'What would you like to have?' Lalit was very solicitous. His friend too.

'C-Coke,' I said, quickly calculating that it was better not to pretend that I drink beer, especially after that disastrous fall in grown-up clothes.

After a while, I was actually relaxing and laughing at all the funny stories the boys narrated.

The evening was flowing pleasantly along. Then the dinner was over. It was still early in the night when Lalit and Bunty brought me safely back and deposited me home.

They must have laughed afterwards at how silly lovestruck schoolgirls can be.

Not very much later, I heard that Lalit was seeing someone.

She was a model, a new girl who had just done the very successful ad for Liril soap.

Bunty, or Ajitabh, strangely turned out to be Amitabh Bachchan's younger brother, who subsequently also got married.

So that, as they say, was that.

A couple of years later, I got married, and the crystal clarity of a sixteen-year-old's recollections dimmed gradually over the years to sepia-tinted images.

———

Before one even knew it, I was seventeen. Not a child any more. School was over.

I got admission in 1972 to Stella Maris College. It was a relief to get in. Even in those less-populated days, it was not easy. I needed to choose my career stream.

It was perhaps a natural choice for a girl with a vivid imagination. So, there I was, doing Fine Arts at the prestigious Stella Maris.

I used to go to college every day in our car with a maid sitting with me at the back. Always. This would puzzle me.

'I don't need Jayanti, Papa.'

'No. She has to go with you.'

'But why?'

'Just. It should not bother you. Just forget she is there and go to college.'

'But Papa ...'

The other new thing was that my size was changing every two or three months. It seemed that my body was being stretched at both ends, which was making me taller every few weeks. Clothes were getting shorter, if not tighter. Everything just fit differently. As my new clothes kept getting stitched, with the maid accompanying me there too, of course, I began to like how I looked. For the first time.

But I kept that a secret because I did not really believe it myself. Except that I did notice a lot of eyes on me. I did not wear low necks. My shirts had sleeves. I wore salwar-kameezes a lot. And yet I had boys craning their necks as I passed. I began to suspect that I might actually be nice-looking.

5

Turning Eighteen

I had already heard about Satinder Bedi. He was four or five years older than me.

I knew the girl he was going around with too. I was told that he was very attractive to women. He was a North Indian Sikh, in Madras.

He was the eldest son. His father had supposedly been very wealthy. It seemed true—he was always driving the latest sports cars. Satinder's, or ST (as he was known), stories were fascinating because they were real.

One day, my parents got a call from some mutual friends saying that Mrs Bedi, ST's mother, was keen to send a marriage proposal for me. My father was taken aback. ST was an eligible boy but I was not yet eighteen, so it was out of the question.

November was coming. It would be my eighteenth birthday very soon.

The Big One, I thought. This means permission to have a party, perhaps! Maybe the weekend after the birthday? I was toying with the date and the guest list for my birthday on a warm October morning when I heard a commotion downstairs, outside.

The Chowkidar was talking torrentially, his voice in a clatter like several kitchen pots. How loud it was! Then I heard my ayah. She was shouting excitedly too outside the house in the driveway. My stomach clenched in alarm. Was everything okay? Mummy? Papa? I threw on a wrap, as my nightie was sheer, and rushed to my balcony. I looked down.

What I saw in the driveway was like a clip from a movie—there he was, Papa, in his lungi and kurta, standing and staring. I turned my gaze towards where he was staring—something huge stood there wrapped in metres of red satin ribbon tied into a spectacular bow. Wrapped in red ribbon was a new white car! On it rested a huge basket with hundreds of red roses—or so it seemed!

I heard the staff saying, 'ST Aiyya, ST Aiyya' many times amongst themselves. I had been gifted a car by my potential husband. I felt like the hundreds of roses—special!

I began to walk down. An excited daze was coming over me.

'Papa?' I said.

He looked annoyed. He took my arm and pulled me inside into his study, away from the stares.

'ST Bedi has sent this birthday present for you!'

I was speechless.

'Oh my God!' I said. But I thought, 'What will my friends say? They'll be proud. No, jealous. We will laugh. I will be such a heroine!'

Papa's words broke through my thoughts. 'It's ridiculous and unacceptable, I'm afraid. These rich, impulsive boys. We are not accepting this for a minute!'

Papa had the car sent back.

———

'Papa,' I said. It was days later. He had started his dinner with his usual glass of beer that accompanied it. This was a good time to talk.

'Hmm?'

'So, you had asked what I want for my eighteenth birthday and now I know what it is.'

'Tell me.'

'I want a party. An eighteenth-birthday party.' I now wonder if I really wanted that party or if I just thought that at eighteen I should be having one.

He heard me out.

'Should be okay,' he said.

I cleared my throat. 'It's ... it'll have to be a mixed party, of course ...'

'You mean boys?'

I nodded my head vigorously. *Yes.*

'No. No boys, that's out.'

'But no one has a party at eighteen with just girls.'

He could not see why this should be a problem. We went back and forth. It was a deadlock.

Ranjit, the son of one of my parents' friends, was staying with us for a few days. He was older than me and was in Madras for a job opportunity. He intervened and managed to convince Papa that this was just how things were nowadays.

'Okay then.' He shrugged. 'Let them come if you think you must. The party time will be from six to eight. Dinner can be served at eight and all the kids can be back safely.'

'Nobody will come to a party at six in the evening, Papa!'

Negotiating each bit of these details, he slowly relented to seven to nine.

It felt like a party from hell. Everybody was scared of my father, of course, because he had a formidable reputation. No one came anywhere near me.

So there Papa was, standing in the large balcony upstairs, looking down at the party taking place below.

The few boys that were brave enough to come were terrified. Once the party was under way, the music needed to be put on and the lights dimmed, but seeing him there did not allow anyone to 'get in the mood', I was told later.

I was most embarrassed. Finally, by nine p.m., there was only me and our house guest Ranjit, with loads of food and cake and the music that we had agonized over. Later, Ranjit confessed that it was the 'scariest birthday party' he had ever attended. Much later, he married a bubbly airhostess working with British Airways, Kavita, and settled in Sri Lanka. We had some wonderful times, but the 'party' was always remembered.

Soon after, Satinder and I met. He arranged for it to happen.

Then he switched on the charm. He was flamboyant, handsome and generous. I already had a father who enjoyed his lifestyle, but ST took it to another level, creating awe wherever he went.

He had always had girlfriends on his sleeve. He was going around with some new girl or the other when we met, but our meeting was special for him, he said.

'You're the girl I have always wanted, Mira. I have waited all my life for you.'

It was so romantic!

I was on a silver cloud, riding the skies. It was dizzy, special. I did not stop to see if this would work. Were we compatible?

All I knew was that if I just said yes, my life would continue in Madras, which was now familiar and comfortable; only, it would get much, much better! I would be looked after, adored, worshipped. Yet I would be free—free to be with a man, free to go to parties, free to dress the way I felt like! I would live in more luxury and abundance than I could ever imagine. And his mother already doted on me. I would be foolish to say no to this chance from heaven.

I was almost an adult. I had adult dilemmas and a child's ignorance. But I could never tell my parents things, discuss, confess to mistakes, confer, experiment.

It would not be easy to describe my father. He had a multilayered personality which, when I see it from a child's perspective, was a secure, safe and loving presence. He was not a good-looking man in the strict sense of the term, but extremely charismatic. He came from a conventional middle-class family and was the first son after three daughters, adored and spoilt by his parents and sisters.

My grandfather, with his intellect and single-minded perseverance as a young boy from a backward district, had joined the Roorkee College of Engineering which he left with distinction. He rose up the ranks to become Chairman of the Central Water and Power Commission of India, and also the Chief Engineer of the Bhakra Nangal Dam project, which was then symbolic of a resurgent India. He was awarded the Padma Bhushan for his services to the country and was also a recipient of the Order of the British Empire.

I remember staying with my grandparents when we were children. My grandfather's style of living was very evocative of who he was—my grandmother had to cook for him every day or he refused to eat! His sense of discipline was apparent in the fact that he would not allow his government car to be used by my grandmother, even if it was to just to go to the market. 'This is only for official work,' he would reprimand her. She would grumble behind his back but never in front of him.

My father, however, was a maverick. He was inordinately generous and loved the good things in life. Fishing, shooting, great food, fine whisky. I had seen him work hard and travel extensively all my life.

He worked for a British company called Blackwood Hodge, which dealt with heavy earth-moving equipment. It was subsequently taken over by the Birlas to become Gmmco, of which he was the President during our years in Madras. However, the love of his life was always my mother, who was the sister of his best friend, Sarabjit, and whom he had known all his growing years. He courted her briefly when he came back from England and they subsequently married. She was a great beauty, and capricious, as most beautiful women are. They were very different temperamentally—she was used to much adulation and he was understated in his displays of affection, so the marriage was always tempestuous.

That was probably why he was always overprotective of us while we were growing up.

I could not grow up gently, protected by a mentoring presence. The unsteadiness of my life growing up went unnoticed in the magic alternate world created by my father for us.

It started with the idea of Cambridge. Papa came up with the idea soon before my seventeenth birthday: 'If you do well in your exams, I will send you to Cambridge to study. You love reading, you write well. History, journalism—whatever you want to do.'

But my thoughts were, *Studying abroad?*

I feared change. Going abroad would be a new, unknown territory.

———

My Dadi was visiting us in those days. My father discussed the marriage proposal with her, saying that obviously, we couldn't accept since I was too young.

'I think it's a very good idea. The earlier Mira settles down, the better. And this is a very good home. They are established. Wealthy. The mother likes Mira a lot. The boy seems so infatuated.'

'Biji, Mira has got into Cambridge. I have made all the arrangements, everything, for that. Let her finish her education. Let her be older at least …'

'Such things don't happen every day. And he's a catch, Chander.'

Papa shook his head. 'No.'

Dadi pushed on, 'And let's not forget, it is best to take a good proposal when it comes.'

'No, no. Mira should study at this age. Marriage is not everything. You leave it to me. If they are so keen, they can wait a couple of years. There's enough time. Mira is not even eighteen and that boy is just twenty-two. What's the hurry? I'll convince them. Nothing for now.'

When Satinder's mother wanted to visit, she was warmly welcomed by my Dadi.

She quickly noticed that Dadi was keen and that what she thought mattered to all of us. 'Biji,' she explained, 'I am a simple woman. I tell the truth. I really like your granddaughter. She will be very happy in our home. That I can assure you.'

Dadi nodded. Mummy said nothing. But Papa said, 'Behenji, thank you for your kind words. We really appreciate your sentiments. But Mira is too young. She has to study. She must complete her education. And Satinder is also so young. What is the hurry for either of them? He has also done his basic college and is probably settling down with work. Let's review things after a few years.'

'Bhaisaab, you don't understand. The hurry is because of his horoscope. It is written he will meet a girl now, at this time. See? He has no father at such a young age!' Mrs Bedi's voice shook. 'That has come true. It was predicted. And now it says that if he doesn't settle down in this short period, he will never settle down. And look at God's grace! He has sent Mira. The boy is so fussy and he adores her. We adore her. What's the problem then? She will live like a queen. What's studying abroad in front of—'

'Behenji, it's just that she has got admission, everything is ready and she is so keen to finish ...'

'No, Papa,' I spoke up. All eyes turned towards me. 'I have really thought about it. I want to get married. I don't want to go to Cambridge.'

Dadi nodded encouragingly.

'But Mira ...' Papa said.

'No. I'm not interested in studying so much. And going so far away.'

Papa looked unsure. He sat down. His hand passed across his forehead in a gesture of helplessness.

Dadi spoke, 'Behenji, my son and daughter-in-law will get back to you very soon. Thank you so much for your proposal. We will get back to you soon.'

After Mrs Bedi left, Papa said, 'Mira, if that's what you say, then beta, we don't have much of a choice. Are you sure this is really your wish? Everything has been taken care of for your studies abroad ...'

'No, Papa. I want to get married.'

My father's protectiveness had gone the other way. I had rebelled against Cambridge just for the sake of it.

Looking back, how could one marry someone that one did not even know at all?

But then I did not even know myself. I did not know who I was.

6

Marriage

The marriage was a series of blurs in technicolour. We had a traditional Hindu ceremony followed by a Sikh one the next morning.

ST had a very close friend, the well-known film star Jeetendra, who danced in full regalia at his baraat, which was quite the highlight in conservative Madras at that time! Then there was the wedding, which stretched on and on, with me in a heavy sari, weighed down with jewellery and an uncomfortable hairdo, which felt like it was full of needles! All I remember after it was done is opening the bedroom door, exhausted, when the last guest had gone. Then I saw that the whole room was filled with gifts!

Instantly, I was on the bed, opening one gift after another.

Everywhere there was wrapping paper, ribbons, confetti and an array of gifts from kitchen sets to linen to crockery, much more exciting when they were wrapped up! Hours must have passed.

I had no idea what time it was and how tired I was. When I woke up the next morning, the bed had been cleared. I was covered with a quilt. ST was fast asleep next to me. He told me later that I had fallen asleep in the middle of the bed with the presents piled up, while in the process of opening the last one!

Then we landed, for what was supposed to be our honeymoon, in Bombay.

It was supposed to be a few days away in Bombay until we could go properly somewhere later. I think we spent three or four days there. We were booked at the Oberoi on Nariman Point.

The first evening, his close friend Jeetendra came over for dinner. Jeetu had brought his girlfriend and wife-to-be, Shobha, for a quiet informal time together.

It should have been a relaxed and pleasant evening. But I was nervous and Shobha was not too forthcoming with this new gauche creature she had to spend the evening with.

The guys were fine. They drank and had fun, and so we ended the evening—the start of many.

After the honeymoon, our real life began. Our house was on Harrington Road in Madras. It was not very far from his mother's house, a bungalow in Adyar. It felt so grown-up to be running the house and doing whatever I wanted in those early days. So many new clothes. And jewellery.

And ST. He was warm and loving. He was also generous. Overwhelmingly generous.

The words 'larger than life' became the leitmotif of my life after I got married. ST's father had died suddenly some years earlier. He had built a number of steel rolling mills in the South after coming from Punjab, through sheer hard work and perseverance. The business was progressing when one day, at the prime of his life, he had a heart attack.

After his father's death, ST had been handed a running business. In those days, money in such a business flowed in like water. There was so much of it that I, or rather we, didn't know how to handle it. I remember an incident from those days. It was when we had returned from our honeymoon a few days earlier.

'Keep this away,' he said to me, handing over a large suitcase.

I looked at it and asked, 'Where are we going?'

'Going? Nowhere. Open it. Go on ...' he said.

I opened it. The whole suitcase was full. Notes. Currency. Clean, crisp hundred-rupee notes. I was in shock. I ran my hands along the bundles, a little dazed. 'It's for you. Spend it.'

'Wow, it's like Monopoly,' I said to myself. My pocket money before I got married was a hundred rupees a month.

It continued for many years—the fawning shopkeepers, the parties, the endless friends who were given so much largesse by him.

The lease of the house at Harrington Road was expiring, so we went to see a beautiful house in the very elite Boat Club area in Adyar.

'Do you like it?' ST asked me.

'It's beautiful,' I said. 'But isn't it too large for us?'

'Nothing but the very best for you,' he said.

We moved into the Adyar house—new furniture, paintings, carpets, silver.

My mother-in-law often came to visit. She was very fond of me. She loved fresh juice. I would make it for her myself whenever she came over. I would show her all my new acquisitions and very often would pick up something for her. I could never understand why she looked sad whenever I did that. She would hold me close and say, 'Wahe Guru, have mercy on these children.'

I was a child of nineteen. It would have helped if I could have grown up double fast. But how does one do that?

As if prompting me in that direction, life threw a new gift at me. I was pregnant within the first year of marriage. Samrath, my beloved son, was born in 1974. He was the centre of our existence. ST was overjoyed.

I have rarely seen Papa as delighted as when Samrath was born. After the delivery itself, Papa started doling out hundred-rupee notes to all the staff in the hospital and then in both our homes. It was sheer joy to see my father genuinely excited. 'I will teach him golf and we'll go fishing and …' Papa's name for him was 'Sam'.

He registered Sam in the very exclusive boarding school of those days, the Doon School, for when he would turn eleven.

However, though now parents, ST and I were both young and inexperienced. Life continued. Untrained to manage the business, inexperienced about the treacheries of people, there was no place to head into but disaster.

I did vaguely realize that to run a business, you could not lead this life of leisure, but there was no reality check. We were in the mid 1970s. It was in some ways an unprecedented time in South India, which was suddenly more exposed than it had ever been. ST had his glamorous film friends; Feroz Khan, the actor and producer, was out of a blockbuster Western—his Stetson hat, gun, horses, hospitality and charm were legendary. This was just after his film *Qurbani* had broken all records. He was very friendly with us and we were all praying for the success of the film, especially after Feroz subjected us to the soundtrack for months on a daily basis! It had to succeed so that we could stop hearing the music, as wonderful as it was!

Our kids were more or less the same age and we used to visit Bangalore, going to his new farmhouse every New Year for the most fabulous parties that only he and his wife Sundari could throw. The most sumptuous food and drink (magnums of Cristal champagne) and always, but always, the most interesting guests. Stunning Parveen Babi in a gold sheath dress and a Shahtoosh shawl. Mayur Madhvani, just married to the gorgeous actress Mumtaz, who was delightfully risqué. Vijay Mallya with his new bride-to-be. Parmeshwar Godrej in a dazzling backless, strapless dress. With Feroz, it was always the world as he saw it—and that was in dramatic 3-D colour. The family had its monopoly of good looks—from the swashbuckling brothers to the beautiful Dilshaad, their only sister.

At that time, ST was also very friendly with the Kapoor family. Randhir Kapoor, or Daboo as he was fondly known, was a good friend and ST was given one of the key distributorships in the South for the Raj Kapoor film *Bobby*, with Rishi Kapoor and Dimple Kapadia, which crossed previous box-office boundaries in India. As always, lavish with his generosity, ST would often send crates of Black Label whisky to make sure his guests were comfortable. Of course, he was probably one of the only few, if not the only person, who did not make money on *Bobby*, because unfortunately he delegated to many others who took advantage of his naïveté.

I remember there was one evening when he called Rishi Kapoor or Chintoo to the Gymkhana Club, the place where everyone converged in the evenings, just before the release of *Bobby*. There was a band and music. Chintoo asked me for a dance, and then another friend came on the floor and then yet another, and suddenly it became a riotously fun evening. He just seemed to be a cool guy with whom we all had a good time. Of course, *Bobby* had not released yet.

The other vivid incident I must recount here is of Rajesh Khanna, and the era that we are talking of is when he was at the height of his superstar status. He was friendly with ST, but they used to generally meet alone with the guys whenever he was in Chennai for a shoot. This suited us till one day when he was going to be there for the premiere of one of his hit films in Chennai. He had told ST, bring your wife if you like for the premiere, and of course I was dying to go. It was a revelation. They were in the car ahead of us, and I was just behind them with two more people in the next car. There seemed to be a cavalcade of cars behind us.

There were people lying on the road blocking the car, women breaking their bangles and smearing blood on their foreheads, and reaching out in hordes to try and touch his car, even the dust below his car tyres! It was quite unbelievable. We finally went back to his suite at the Chola Hotel and he changed into what was obviously a trademark silk lungi–kurta. There were already three or four guys in the room waiting for him, and ST gestured that we should leave.

'Will you have something?' Rajesh Khanna asked.

'Have to get back to my son now, but this was the experience of a lifetime. Thank you so much.'

'I believe your father also stays in the same suite?'

'Yes, he does,' I said.

'Good. I hope it will be as lucky for him as it has been for me.'

I smiled. 'I hope so.'

I remember him as being exceptionally charming, and the epitome of a 'star'.

———

One clear memory of the time I got married was when my mother-in-law told my father shortly before the actual ceremony: *'Bhaisaab, ek commitment chahiye.'*

My father looked askance but said, 'Anything at all, ji, you only have to say it.'

'My daughter, Anita, ST's sister, has no father, as you know. I would like you to promise me that you will find a good husband for her.'

My father's response was immediate. 'It is now completely my responsibility, ji. Don't worry at all. I will find her a suitable husband.'

She smiled at him and said, *'Hun mein nu koi fikar nahi.'*

As expected, it became one of Papa's priorities. Sometime later, I came to know from my mother that he had spoken to some close friends of theirs, Nikki and Karnail Singh. Uncle Karnail was the Chief Commissioner of Income Tax, and I remember him as being a tall, imposing man. Nikki Aunty had been in college with Mummy. The couple had two good-looking sons, whom we had known since childhood. 'Oh, really?' I said. 'Who is he thinking of? Nechal or Sadeev?'

Nechal was like his father, responsible and disciplined. Sadeev was more fun-loving and flamboyant. I still remember when Sadeev had bought a racy little yellow sports car—I must have been in my teens and he was slightly older. He had parked it in our garage for a few days, and I was awed by the car. I never quite figured out whether it was because there was not enough space for another car in their home, or the fact that he didn't want his parents to know about it!

I was sure my father meant to suggest Nechal for Anita. As we found out later, that's exactly how it was. The families had so much regard for each other that Nechal's parents did not question the fact that my father had thought Anita a suitable bride for their son.

Papa used to travel quite frequently to Delhi in those days and had arranged with my mother-in-law to fix a meeting in his hotel suite with the boy's family and ours. Everything went well. I think Anita, who had a very sheltered upbringing, saw the tall handsome sardar and was quite smitten! That continues to this day.

Nechal had joined the police force. For many years, Anita and he were transferred to various places in the back of beyond. I did not know that Jhumri Telaiya actually existed until they were transferred there!

There were many postings—the most recent being Jammu and Kashmir—and finally they were back in Delhi. It has been almost thirty years since they were married, and Anita now had this sprawling home in Lutyens' Delhi, with beautiful gardens filled with gorgeously exotic flowers. It did cross my mind at some point occasionally that Nechal must be in some very important position, but it never really came up between us, strange as that may sound! We only realized that he had been the very prestigious Chief of the Intelligence Bureau after he finally retired!

By the time we roller-coastered our way to 1976, there seemed to be no money and no business to generate it from, in real terms.

When I did finally get some understanding of the situation, it was already too late. The factories shut down one by one.

It was in the same year that our second child came into the world—a baby girl. I was twenty-one and Sam was two. ST and I named her Diviya. It meant the Divine Light. She had huge eyes and unquestioningly followed her brother everywhere.

Those were tumultuous times. There was very little money—sometimes none.

I took to selling the silver one by one, pretending everything was fine and also pretending to myself that when the money would come, I would buy it back.

Slowly, the time came when we had to move out of the Boat Club Road house and into the house where his mother and brother stayed, to cut down on our expenses.

We lived upstairs and they downstairs. ST used to have outbursts of anger. Gradually, these outbursts happened more and more often. The drinking also increased.

———

The children were maybe four and two when we met Kenny and Ponchie. Kenny was the son of Sardar Raunaq Singh, well known as one of the giants of industry in India. He was seen as a great entrepreneur who had created an empire out of nothing.

In Madras too, so far from Punjab, the Sikh community regarded him with great respect, even awe.

Kenny was very much a Punjabi—loud, generous and loving the good life. He had a party at home almost every night. There usually was a most interesting mix of characters each time.

Ponchie, his wife, was the opposite—simple and unpretentious. Many times, when a party was going on downstairs, she would be upstairs in her room watching TV or just reading. We used to spend a lot of time together.

Their children were almost the same age as ours.

I remember how we decided to learn painting one day. We both bought watercolours, canvasses and books on how to paint. We would take the children, drive down to the beach in Mahabalipuram, put up our canvases and paint, engrossed for hours.

We gave our paintings to our fathers. Both fathers gave the paintings pride of place in their homes. With parents, you could not be quite sure what they actually thought of them, but both Ponchie and I were told that they were beautiful and that we were so talented!

It was a time when we were young and uncomplicated. Everyone knew everyone. We met almost every day in our own or someone else's home. Ponchie used to call me over every time her father-in-law was in town.

'Father (as they called him) loves to chat with you, so please come.'

Raunaqji used to tell me the story of how he started on a bicycle and went on to build his business by selling car spare parts. I would listen as carefully every time as if it was the first. He was very fond of me. And I of him.

This life continued for many years. We could never have imagined then that ST and I would separate, that I would be orphaned at such an early stage in my life, that Kenny and Ponchie would get divorced and he would die early of a heart attack, that life would change dramatically.

In 1979, my parents moved back to Delhi. They left without any idea of what I was going through. I was desperate that Papa should not find out. I never wanted him to know. In a way it was better that they went so far away. Once my parents settled down, I did go to Delhi but it was not very often.

Till they were in Madras, Biji used to come and stay as she always did. She was extremely fond of ST and he of her.

I loved her with a child's intensity. I trusted her deeply. Yet I never told her about our problems. How could I? How much it would have hurt her to know the truth about her favourite grandchild!

She enjoyed being with both the great-grandchildren, Samrath and Diviya, but there was something about Diviya's not-very-expressive personality that drew Biji's protectiveness.

Her role in my life was changing. Already, with my parents' shift to Delhi, I knew that Biji would no longer visit Madras. Then she began to have back problems. It was only much later, after much suffering, that my uncle, Jiti Mamu, discovered that it was cancer. I made a few visits to Bombay to be with her.

By then she was in hospital. Often, I would stay back with her there. It was very difficult to see her the way she was, when throughout her life she had been so meticulous about everything. She could not speak. She did not seem to be really conscious. But I know she was aware I was there. Because she already knew what she meant to me in any case. And that was what mattered. And then, with the general drifting away of my support systems, Biji too passed away in 1979. My sweet, dearly beloved Biji.

———

After the high life beyond my dreams, the downhill swing was equally bad.

Frustration and the inability to address his issues blanked ST's thinking, and he would find solace in drinking sprees. Everything became an excuse in that condition.

Our social life was such that often I would be at the receiving end of admiration and compliments. Any attention would infuriate ST—it was all my fault, he would say. He would then become another person, lashing out physically at night and then regretting it, begging to be forgiven the next morning, only to repeat the same thing, day after day. Life was a difficult pretence—pretending things were fine for the children, in front of my parents and society at large.

And there was no money for anything. They say that when life gives a problem, some power greater than the problem gives us strength, if only we are able to receive it. It must have been that power which watched over us. What else was keeping me alive from one day to the next? I do not have any other answer.

———

I think it must have been 1981. Papa was on a work trip to Madras. He decided to surprise me with a visit. That was when he saw the bruises on my face and arms. He was shocked.

I told him that I had fallen in the bath. But he knew. He called ST and said everything else was acceptable but not this.

He was deeply repentant as always. He swore to my father that it would not happen again. But for the first time, I was terrified of him. I cried and cried.

And Papa brought me back to Delhi with him.

Till today, I have no derogatory words to say about ST, and still maintain that he was warm and caring when he was himself. We did not fight. It was what happened when he drank.

But gradually the physical and psychological violence was becoming impossible to live with. It became a question of survival.

However, at that time, my stay in Delhi turned out to be temporary.

Hope moves mountains; ST came to Delhi a week later and begged me to come back. He said I had to give him another chance and that he could not live without me.

I desperately wanted to believe him. I went back.

7

My Mother's Death

Soon after, I heard that my sister Choti was being serenaded by Gokul Tandon, I was thrilled. Gokul was the son of close friends of my parents, and he seemed to be the ideal match for her.

Choti got married to Gokul in 1982. Everyone was happy with the alliance. There were many celebrations, and everyone enjoyed the festivities with much fun, song and dance. But every time I visited Delhi, once or twice a year, Choti seemed to be partying too much.

She was still gorgeous and Gokul was as besotted as before, but apparently not strong enough to contain her. I was getting feedback that the fun evenings they had were getting out of control. Choti, I was told, used to sometimes drink too much, but it was always passed off as 'she was in a party mood and got smashed'. No one drew that much-needed line. And it was hidden from Papa.

One day, Choti was unwell and had to be taken to the doctor—she came out of the clinic with a wonderful surprise.

'I'm pregnant,' she announced. We were delighted.

However, in the more unhappy mess of memories of those days, there stands out this one worst memory of all.

It was late afternoon. I still remember the phone ringing for a long time.

'Hello?'

It was a trunk call. A lightning call from Papa's office, in the time of no mobiles, looking for him.

They urgently wanted to know his whereabouts. Papa was in Madras for some work.

'What is the matter?' I asked.

'There was a call from his residence. Your mother's room is locked. There's no reply and they are unable to open the door!' It was his secretary.

'I'll try to contact him,' I said. My stomach tightened even more. I felt the ice-cold grip of fear.

He was at some meeting.

I got through but they had already spoken to him and he said he would call back. I called the house in Delhi. There seemed to be mayhem. The door to my mother's room was broken down. I could not piece together the terrifying reality as no one gave me a coherent explanation. I was told that she had been taken to a hospital.

My father and I took the morning flight to Delhi. We did not know the details till we arrived. It was a blur.

It seemed like we were in someone else's horror story. There had been a robbery. The door was found locked. It seemed to be an inside job. Her locker was open. There had been a struggle and she had been killed.

The days passed with the cremation and prayers, the people coming in; some who wanted to hear the story again and again: 'What was the weapon?' 'How many times was she stabbed?' 'What was stolen?'

'Are you sure it was the one who ran away? Maybe it's someone still in the house.' The police came in and kept coming for many months. Sometimes they would have a lead in Karnataka, and my father would make arrangements for them to go there. Sometimes they had a lead in Kashmir, sometimes in Mumbai. They wanted money, and sometimes a car, to investigate. It went on and on—the leads never materialized into anything.

One day, I told my father that we had to stop. 'What will we gain if we find the person? Let it go.' He had aged in those months. There were streaks of grey in his hair that had not been there before.

————

Choti's daughter, Sagarika, was born in 1983, a few months after Mummy's death. She was a beautiful baby.

No one could understand what made Choti unhappy at that time. She was arrestingly attractive, married to a loving man, had a good family, a baby ... no lack of the material things in life.

We started the rounds of trying to find the problem with doctors and psychiatrists and had no idea that that was going to be routine for us for the next fifteen years—correction, routine for *me*.

8

Back Home

After Mummy's death, I began to visit Delhi more frequently. Every six to eight months, during the children's holidays, I would spend a week or ten days there with my father. It was a painful time, but it was also when I began trying to catch up with my Delhi friends. Adita was one of them.

We were in Connaught Place, shopping and spending time together.

It is still so clear in my memory—we were waiting at the red light near the large jewellery store Tribhovandas Bhimji Zaveri when a Mercedes-Benz drew up next to us and also waited for the light to turn green. The man in the car turned and saw us. He waved at me. I waved back. When we finally drove off, Adita asked, 'Who was that?'

I said, 'That's Sanjay Bhaskar.'

'How do you know him?'

I looked at Adu. 'We know him quite well socially. He has a set-up in Madras—a large factory just outside the city. So, he's there a lot. After all, he's a bachelor. And you just saw him ... what d'you expect!' I smiled.

'So, he's not married ...'

'No,' I said. I looked at Adita. She was lovely, young and very bright. Her parents were getting restless, trying to find the right boy for her to settle down with. Each time Adita would say 'He's not this' or 'He's not that'. And here she was, looking curious and interested!

Sanjay was young and rather good-looking and had a great sense of humour. Why had I not thought of him before?

'I didn't think of it earlier. If you want, I can find out how to contact him. Easily. Just that I don't have his number right now, but that's not a problem.'

'He looks interesting,' Adu said. 'Maybe we can fix to meet?'

'Sure!' I said.

I called someone who called someone and finally I got Sanjay Bhaskar's office number. And then I called him. He was in his office. And he was quite surprised when I called.

'Hi Bugam!' I said. He was called Bugam by friends.

'Hi! How's everything? ST with you?' he said, pleasantly cautious.

'No, he is not. Are you free this evening? Come over for a drink?'

Later, he said that he was quite blown away by what he thought were my advances!

'Yes, sure! Would love to.'

Bugam came home in a crisp white kurta-pyjama. My father offered him a drink. He accepted, a bit bewildered as to what was to happen next, but quite relaxed generally.

We were all chatting away and then we both looked at the door because in walked Adita, as if it was just one of her usual visits.

She lived next door, a few houses from us. We had been very careful to make it seem casual.

I looked at her. I couldn't help seeing her from the eyes of a young man—she looked gorgeous. She wore a white chikan kurta. She was simple and unaffected. And with her long silky hair, her slim figure and her beautiful face, she would take anybody's breath away.

Bugam fell madly in love with her that moment.

We spent a great evening and had dinner. After dinner he asked Papa if he could take us both for an ice cream, and we went. After the ice cream, he dropped me home at the gate and drove off to drop Adita just further down the road. Papa was at our gate, looking at Bugam's car as it drove away. They stopped for a while at her house, and then both of them drove off again. He was furious!

'Where could he have taken Adita? He should have dropped her home. What'll I tell Adita's father?'

The next morning, Adita came across.

'Well, that's it. That's the guy I want to marry.' And that was it. The perfect match. They did get married. It has now been maybe thirty-five years. Till today, on their anniversary every year, I get flowers saying 'thank you'.

———

Mummy must have been in her late forties when she died. My father always had an inexplicable deep love for her. A year later, I found his letter to her in a drawer in his bedroom.

It must have reached Mummy just a little before her death. He was abroad on a work trip when he wrote it. He wrote to her of the wonderful things that he had planned they would do together in their lifetime. All the things that he wanted to do at work and yet had not been able to. All he needed, he had written, was his Raj by his side. He wanted her to make the effort to be the person whom he had met and loved. The person with whom he had had such wonderful times; the person that she still potentially was.

My own pain and shock at Mummy's death were bad enough. But it was compounded for me by imagining how lonely and stressed Papa must have been.

What little idea I had of the road ahead! Life is kind. It does not let us see the future.

———

I was twenty-eight years old when I decided to come back to my father's home. The marriage was over. I had given it my very best shot. Being alive and safe was now a priority after the way things had turned out. I packed my bags and those of my children. The children loved their father. Samrath was ten and Diviya was eight. I told them.

'We cannot stay here any longer. It is better for us and for your father.' They had seen my bruises, so this was not news.

'But Papa?' They both looked at me, questions in their sad eyes.

'Don't worry. Papa can come and see you any time he wants. I'll try to send you to Doon like Bara Papa and Diviya to Welham's which is right there too, and for girls. You will have friends and games in boarding school.'

Diviya's short hair framed her large, worried eyes.

'Where will we go from here?' Sam asked. How small he looked in his shorts and blue Benetton T-shirt! I felt something tear and hurt within me. I talked to them many times to reassure them.

'We are going to Bara Papa in Delhi.'

Slowly, they understood. And accepted. Children can be very grown-up. More than adults sometimes.

Change, even change meant for the better, is frightening. I was hollow with it. Like a ghost walking.

Two days before we left, Diviya came to me.

'Mom,' she said, not moving.

'Yes, darling?'

'I'm staying with Papa. I'll look after him ...'

'No, Diviya! He can't look after you! You know he is not well at all.'

'I'll stay with Chacha and Chachi and I'll look after Papa.'

Both the children loved ST. I tried to get everyone else to talk to her and explain the situation. But Diviya just did not relent. She was adamant. I was desolate.

'Diviya, who'll look after me? Who'll be there for me?' I pleaded, fear and grief making my voice shake.

But Diviya said, 'Mamma, Samu will go with you and he'll look after you.'

Her Chacha and Chachi said that I couldn't forcibly change a child's decision to stay with her father even as I begged her to reconsider. ST did not say a word.

Two days later, Samu and I left. We turned and looked at that house in Adyar as we drove to the airport. It had turned from our home into just a house like any other on the street, with that one difficult decision to separate.

That's all it had taken for nothing to remain the same. My daughter was not in my care. My husband was not my husband. Nothing made sense. I felt raw and numb at the same time.

I remember that drive to the Madras airport. Vividly. Little Sam was with me—my consolation and my heartache. We can take our pain. But when it comes to the children, it can feel perilous.

We came to Delhi to my father's house in Panchsheel Park. There was a hole where my heart should have been.

But the sheer safety every evening Samu and I felt, knowing we were at home, brought relief. I managed to start sleeping again—a sleep constantly prickling with thoughts of Diviya. I knew she would be safe. ST was never violent with her. But logic is not always enough.

In Delhi I could see problems arising between Choti and Gokul. Shagu grew up in front of me from the time I returned. She was a baby when I came. I spent a lot of time with her.

By the time she was close to a year, we had become very attached to each other. She lived with her paternal grandparents and was understandably spoiled by them. However, with no one to be strict with her, she became increasingly defiant.

My father continued to travel frequently for his work. With Mummy gone and his constant travelling, Papa had employed a housekeeper for the Delhi home, Mrs Simon.

You could say that she was an advanced version of our earlier Prem Singh. And a glimmer of the old, relaxed Delhi days was returning. Mrs Simon was a treasure, found after my mother died. She had responded to an ad that was put out by Papa's Madras office. She was in her late thirties or early forties at the time. She was a widow and came from Madurai. Her brother-in-law worked in Papa's office in Chennai.

She was an educated, simple and God-fearing Christian. She woke up at 4.30 every morning. Before any of us were up, the house was humming into readiness for our day.

For the first time since I can remember, all of Papa's needs were being attended to and provided for—different breakfasts of his liking, fresh flowers in all the rooms, delicious meals, neatly pressed shirts and trousers.

Mrs Simon welcomed me and Sam with warmth. She supervised homework, laughed and told stories, managed our clothes, placed a hot-water bottle in our beds in winter, changed our towels twice a day in summer … Our house was now a warm, well-run home. I remember her being tall and fair, dressed in white saris with thin borders. She wore her hair in a tight plait with a flower tucked into it on one side.

She was, it would seem, born for loving service, unfailingly there in the background, efficient, warm, caring.

We all loved her. Over time we got to know of her past, which had been a difficult one. Maybe that and her prayers had made her who she now was. My father too wanted to do something for her, he said, so that she would not need to be dependent on anyone for the rest of her life.

We were beginning to relax. Friends were beginning to come over, stay like old times, and things were slowly getting better.

———

It was 1983, the year of the World Cup. We all went to London—so many friends and the madness of cricket, of which I know nothing. It was a crazy time—actually, the first time that I could let my hair down. After the spectacular win, all of us, including Papa, celebrated like every other Indian across the world.

We had met with Kapil Dev before the match but the subsequent hysteria that was generated after was beyond anything we could have imagined. Kapil got the status of a demigod. Romi, his wife, went on to become a dear friend, and remains so to this day.

I remember that when Romi had a very difficult pregnancy, my friends Guddu, Wanti and I used to meet her regularly for lunches. She was on bed rest for almost nine months but when Amiya was born, it was all worth it. She was the most delightful child who had the best of both her parents.

It was also 1983 when Shagu turned one. I went over to Choti's and we decorated the house with balloons and streamers. There was a '1' on her beautiful pink cake. Everything had to be pink—Shagu's favourite colour. It still is.

My father had just come back from an overseas trip. He was there for Shagu's birthday as he had planned to be.

———

April 1984. An unforgettable April of my life. The night before we had gone to have dinner with Sadeev, an old friend of ours, and his wife, and had a very pleasant evening.

It was early in the morning. My old friend, Radha, was staying with me for a few days and we were sharing the bedroom. Suddenly, there was a crash outside the room.

Mrs Simon had dropped the tray with Papa's tea. The bedroom door was open, and she was standing in the doorway.

'Mira Ma'am, quickly come. Saab is not okay.'

She was shaking with fear. I ran into the bedroom. Papa was sitting up in bed propped up against his pillows, talking on the phone, it seemed. Going closer, I saw that the phone had dropped from his hand and he was lying back on the pillow.

I couldn't understand. Was he resting? He was wearing a white kurta with a deep blue cotton lungi, his favourite.

Radha came running behind me.

Mrs Simon was sobbing, of all things!

Radha said, 'I'm calling the doctor!' and ran out of the room.

I said to Mrs Simon, 'Please stop crying.' That was scaring me. 'He's sleeping. I'm going to wake him up.'

I sat on the bed and held his hand and said, 'Papa, get up. Please get up, we had such a nice dinner yesterday … must tell you.'

He was not moving.

'Papa, get up.' But now I was screaming, 'Get up, don't sleep for so long, please get up.'

His hand dropped from my grip. But he looked fine. There was a faint smile on his face, and he looked like he would just say, 'What's the matter with all of you?'

I was told later that I wouldn't leave him. The doctors came, closed his eyes, injected me with a sedative, took me away.

By this time, the news had spread and there were many people around and everything after that was a daze. He had died. The world … had ended.

My greatest support system, the only one whom I could rely on, had gone. There was no one—Mummy had died a year before, and my father had brought me back home after he saw my precarious state. He had said that I should not worry at all. He would send me abroad to study and that my children would be looked after.

I was completely devastated. The days after he died were a blur. Our Indian practices, with everyone coming in and the endless rituals, numb the mind, as they are probably meant to do. I stopped praying and became bitter and resentful towards God, my mainstay all these years. He could not be real. He did not exist.

'How could you let me down?' I asked Babaji. 'You don't exist. I will never pray again.'

The days passed with the Akhand Paath and the Kirtans and the people, people and more people—all those who loved him and had their own particular affinity with him.

One day there was a Kirtan with a Paathi, a priest, who had the most beautiful face and voice. He looked like Guru Nanakji. I sat through it in my veil of misery. Suddenly, at the end, he came up to me.

'Biba,' he said. 'May I say something to you?'

'Yes.' I looked up at him, not really paying attention.

'I know what you have been through, but you are very selfish. Only thinking of yourself.'

I sat up. I couldn't believe he said that after all the sympathy I had been receiving. 'I don't understand.'

'It's very simple. You are blaming God for taking your father away. He gave him to you for many years. You have amazing memories of your life with him but you do realize that He could have taken your father away much earlier, at any time. Instead of thanking Him for having given you so much joy with your father, you are blaming Him. That is selfish.'

What he said had a profound effect on me. It changed the way I thought. It also gave me the courage to decide that I have to carry on, for the sake of my children.

And for what Papa would have wanted.

———

When my father died, the realization of the hard facts of life actually hit me: the first was that there was no will.

He was only fifty-two, unprepared to die, and it was so sudden.

In real terms that meant there was no access to any money as I came to know that accounts are frozen in the absence of a will.

Again, everything was the company's—the cars, drivers, servants. The company was good to us—he had been very respected and loved in the organization—but, though in gentle terms, there was a deadline.

I had no idea about what to do. At the time there was estate duty. The procedure of applying for a probate of the will was long and tedious. Copies of his death certificate, my mother's death certificate, affidavits, guarantees, proof to show that we were the only heirs. I went for advice to my father's Charted Accountant and the process of trying to decipher what to do started. It was a mind-numbing exercise. Finally, I had it done.

Basically, it was our house in Panchsheel and the land at Rishikesh that we had not seen. There was hardly any money.

We lived a very good life but he was scrupulously honest and there was no money taken under the table.

That was how it was and quite frankly, in retrospect, I would not have preferred it any other way.

9

Arranging for Survival

It was 1985. Choti's husband filed for a divorce.

The papers said that Gokul felt that they were incompatible and wanted an amicable divorce.

After her divorce, Choti's responsibility came onto Jiti Mamu, by default his wife Kamma Aunty, and me.

I must mention here that Kamma Aunty was a very important thread throughout my growing-up years. She is what I look at as the Ardhangani or the other half of my Jiti Mamu. She was the most incredible wife and, more importantly, she navigated her life to flow with his. She was always beautifully turned out, her home was impeccable and her attention to detail evident at every step.

Choti, I think was the only time she was completely out of her depth!

Jiti Mamu was a meticulous man who took his responsibility very seriously. He oversaw all the doctors' meetings with me, kept Choti's accounts, disagreed with me when he thought my stubbornness not to sell the house would be detrimental to her. She was placed under specialized care.

After that, for a few months, she would promise to be fine and we would take her out. But then we would go through the same cycle again.

It took its toll on all of us, in lesser or greater degree.

Then there was the question of survival. My father had died suddenly. He had not made any arrangements for after his death. All our supposed well-wishers told me to sell Panchsheel and get two small flats for Choti and myself. The constant question was: 'How will you maintain the house?'

I do remember that I had no idea how, but I only knew that I could not sell it.

My father had used his provident fund to build the house—something I found out only after he died—and I was determined not to sell if I could avoid it. All that remained to be seen was how it could happen and never *if* it could happen.

Despite all odds, I decided, therefore, that the only way to keep Panchsheel was to build upstairs; it was a single-storey house. There was an old plan which had two bedrooms upstairs. This plan had been passed but not built. So, I thought both of us could have one bedroom each on a floor built upstairs and I could give out the downstairs on rent.

This arrangement would save the house and also create an income for us.

The idea was fairly simple. That is where it started. And also ended, apparently. Jiti Mamu, my greatest confidant, lived next door. When I told him about this idea, he thought I was mad.

He said, 'Are you crazy? Where will you get the money to build? And you think building is a joke? You have to take care of the children. Choti is still not completely stable. Who will look after her and the kids?'

I did not want to argue but I had made up my mind.

First was to arrange the money to build. I spoke to a friend who knew someone in Indian Bank.

He arranged the meeting.

I met the Manager and told him how I saw things, ending with, 'If I build, I can give the downstairs on rent and save the house. If you lend me the money, I will pay you back from the rent.'

'What guarantee will I have if you can't pay back the bank?' said the Manager after my hastily rehearsed speech.

I had no guarantee—the papers were not yet mutated in our names. But I said that I would write and give him any undertaking he wanted.

He said, 'How will you build? Do you know anyone?'

I said, 'No. But I will find someone to build.'

After many meetings, he finally sanctioned me the money to build, saying that Indian Bank would pay the builder directly to the limit of six lakh rupees and I would have to give an undertaking for the rent pledged to the bank until we paid back the amount and interest.

I agreed.

A few weeks later, I saw that there was some construction going on a few houses down the road.

I went there and asked, 'Who is building this house?'

The man at the site said, 'The contractor's name is Avtar Singh.'

The next day I went back. There was a man who was just leaving on a scooter. Avtar Singh. I stopped him.

'Sat Sriakal, ji. I need to ask you for a favour,' I said. 'I have to build on top of my house and I need a contractor.'

I think he was taken aback.

'Where?' he said, also coming straight to the point.

I said, 'Just next door. Can you come and see it?'

He came. I told him what the story was in detail, and also that I had got the money from the bank and that it had to be done quickly so we could pay them back.

He said, 'Wahe Guru has sent you to me, so I will do it.'

That was it. That's how we started building.

It was harder than it seemed.

With Mrs Simon helping me to hold the fort at home, everything was focused on building the house. No experience, no money, but it was the only way. And it had to be done.

Adita and Bugam were a huge support. It was Bugam who sent his trusted man Jaswant Singh to supervise the work; he used to come once every few weeks to check the quality of the construction.

It was coming together.

———

Once, while the construction was going on, there was an unexpected period of rain.

I had a friend over from abroad. Andrew was an Englishman, very proper. At the first downpour that day, the rain poured through the cracks and gaps in the roof. The house was flooded. For many weeks, Mrs Simon put assorted buckets and pots under the leaks in different rooms and it stayed like that.

I remember, one day, when the incongruity of the situation hit us— the house dotted with the cooking pots and the different-coloured buckets with the orchestra of drops playing for us—we laughed and laughed till tears were rolling down our cheeks. Andrew said, 'I don't think life will ever be quite as melodramatic as this, Mira, whatever happens!'

Now when I think back, the construction of the first floor was quite astounding.

There was no way it could have got done except with Divine Intervention!

———

It is impossible to think of my adventures with the first floor without remembering my glamorous, beautiful friend Anita Khan. She called me up one day during that phase.

'Hi, Mira! I'm coming to Delhi soon. Can I come and stay with you?'

'Of course!' I said, though I explained what was happening was difficult.

We gave her a warm welcome, but times were tough. We gave her a bedroom which had no heating and a bathroom which had sporadic hot water. It was winter in Delhi.

In the morning, she would come out of her room for tea, her teeth chattering, wearing all the clothes she had brought to keep warm. We would laugh because there was nothing to say.

In fact, we laughed a lot at whatever was happening each day—the day's surprises, the freezing house, the leaking roof, everything. Nothing can explain that phase. We were in fairly penury-stricken circumstances but we had some wonderful times. Anita stayed two weeks with us.

Later, I stayed with her in London and we remembered the crazy, fun days. Today, as a princess in her beautiful palace, these are many memories to remember with a smile.

———

Finally, the first floor was almost ready. Now came the next part: we would have to give the downstairs area on rent to start paying for the loan.

Everyone I spoke to said, 'You have to be very careful, because if you give it to someone, how can you be certain that they will give it back? No one is reliable.' And so on and so forth.

I decided not to listen to anyone, sit down on my own and think rationally. I thought, 'What would be the ideal situation? Who is the ideal tenant I would like to give it to?'

There were no answers coming to my mind. Much soul-searching later it came as a flash—what would be the safest? The American Embassy? ... How would I even get to the American Embassy? There was no sense in talking to anyone since all I would get would be the same: 'What is wrong with you? Do you really think you can do this on your own?'

So I decided to get the telephone directory and look up the American Embassy's number. There was one. I dialled it with trepidation.

'May I speak to someone in charge of your Housing?' I asked. I was asked to hold, and then put through.

'Yes, how may I help?' It was a pronounced American accent.

'I have a ground-floor house in Panchsheel Park that I would like to give on rent to your embassy and I wanted to know how to go about it,' I said all in one breath.

'Is it an independent house?' Okay, he had not hung up.

'Well almost. I live upstairs, but I live alone and it's more or less independent.'

'I'm really sorry but the American Embassy does not take houses, which are not completely independent. Because of strict security issues.'

I was very disappointed. But I was determined to give it another try.

'Look, even if you don't take it, would you come by and have a look?'

He hesitated. 'Well, we do have a few houses in Panchsheel Park and I'm visiting the area the day after tomorrow, so maybe I can drop by.'

'Please, please do. And maybe you could have a cup of coffee with me,' I said to him, wanting him to see how separate the downstairs area was.

We fixed the meeting the following day. I spent an anxious two days before we met, rehearsing what I would say and praying to Babaji that if He had brought me till here, He had to see it through.

It was eleven in the morning—the appointed time. The Embassy Official came in exactly on time.

I came out and saw him. I was in shock.

The 'American' who had been speaking to me was actually an immaculate Sardar in a business suit! A Sikh with a white beard and white turban, and an American accent!

I said, 'Oh my God! Sat Sriakal!'

'Sat Sriakal,' he said. 'What's the problem?'

I proceeded to tell him in great detail, explaining how I had found his number and my process of elimination.

'The American Embassy unfortunately does not take a joint property because of security issues,' he repeated.

I showed him the separate entrances and anything else I could think of. I said, 'I can give you references if you need them.' I was almost in tears as I could feel it going nowhere.

He looked at me. 'Leave it with me. I can't promise but I will see what I can do.'

He was a Godsend. He eventually went out of his way to make it all happen despite the obvious odds and the American Embassy did finally take our ground floor on rent.

The timing for such additional income was providential.

———

My niece Anita came into my life by default. She lived in London with her parents and was a rather rebellious teenager, who they thought should get schooled in India, where she would be more in touch with the culture of her country. She got into Woodstock School, Mussoorie, and since I was the only person they knew in India, I became her guardian.

Anita was a gorgeous sixteen-year-old. Warm, bubbly, affectionate and of course, completely impetuous! It was the time I was staying in Panchsheel before Sam went to boarding school, and we were all in various stages of struggle, learning to cope with being alone.

Anita was a bright light. 'Mira Aunty, I have a brilliant idea!' she would say and let me in on yet another scheme. There was always a new boy she had a crush on, and there were always plenty of them who had a crush on her. The schemes were always crazy and, needless to say, great fun and often, Mrs Simon would hold her head in her hands in exasperation. The children became, of course, great followers of any of Anita Didi's latest exploits!

I remember, one time when she was in school. Her school did not allow anyone other than the guardian to bring the students down during their holidays. I, for some crucial reason, was unable to go to Mussoorie on that day. We were all distraught on how to do this. Finally, Anita had another idea. 'I have it, Aunty. Let's make Mrs Simon go up. I can say she is my guardian!'

'That may not be such a bright idea, Anita. What if someone asks for something? How can we pretend she is me?'

'Don't worry, I will be waiting. I will say my Aunt is in a hurry to get back, and we have to leave immediately. We will rush out.'

I was already guilty about not being able to go up to get her, knowing exactly what it felt like to come home from boarding school, so I explained the plan to Mrs Simon.

Mrs Simon was terrified. 'No, ma'am. How can I pretend to be you? No one will believe it. We can all go to jail, ma'am …'

Anyway, we all worked on her and finally, on the day, Mrs Simon, wearing one of my trademark cotton saris, left for Mussoorie in the car. I believe she prayed all the way there with her rosary, muttering 'God save me' at intervals, was propelled to the school gates by Moti, our driver. There, she was grabbed by Anita who said, 'My darling Mira Aunty, I know you have to go quickly. Bye everyone', and bundled back into the car. Moti drove off instantly, much like the driver of a burglary getaway car, which I think was his secret ambition. So, the deed was done.

After it was over, Mrs Simon recollected it as a thrilling undercover mission.

Many episodes occurred, too numerous to mention, but having her there with me brightened the monotony and realities of my life in those years. When she finally had to go back to London, we were both in tears.

———

Sam had, of course, been registered to the Doon School. Through everything, I was determined that he would go. Now, he was twelve years old. It was time for his entrance exam.

In Madras, there was no Hindi in his school syllabus, and to learn the language was an uphill task. He failed the exam. I was devastated. Lalit Thapar, a very close friend of my father's from their schooldays, was the Chairman of the Board at that time. I went to him and pleaded to get Sam a retrial. He got one.

Then began the studying for the exam. Sam would get up in the morning and have to study. I would sit with him and go through the books day after day. Mrs Simon would keep a strict vigil.

One day I came into the room and he was studying as usual, except I could see something behind the book. I went behind him. I couldn't believe it. It was a comic.

I was livid with him. It was the first time he got a slap from me.

'How could you do this to me?' I was sobbing with anger and frustration.

He looked at me. And then he cried too. After a moment he said, 'Mamma, I promise you I will pass my exams.' After that he studied on his own.

The retrial date came. He gave the exam.

'How did it go?' I asked.

'Fine.'

'What is fine? Did you find the questions difficult?'

'No. Fine.'

Finally, the day came when the results were to be announced. I couldn't sleep the night before.

Early in the morning, we started checking for the lists. Someone said they were out.

I kept trying the school but the lines were constantly busy.

I ran next door to my Mama's house and told my cousin Vikram to keep trying as well. I gave him Sam's registration number. I ran back and tried from my phone.

Sometime later, Vikram rushed across. 'Miru, I got through to the school. Congratulations. Sam's name is on the list.'

'Are you sure? You gave the right number?' I repeated it twice.

'I'm sure. He's in,' Vicky repeated. I hugged him and burst into tears.

Sam came into my room and saw me crying. 'Mamma, I'm so sorry … I tried very hard … I'm very sorry.'

Through my tears I held him. 'No, no. These are tears of joy. You've got into the school.'

The relief was overwhelming. I went to my father's photograph. 'Papa, he's going to school. Just like you wanted.'

After that I got the long lists of what had to be taken to the school. The trunks of warm clothes, uniforms and so on. I had not envisaged this expenditure and was at a loss as to how this would be done. Then I had a brainwave.

I still had the wedding set that my parents had given me when I got married—it would be put to the best use for this. And it was.

Then came the difficult part. Leaving Sam at the school. He had never been away from me. It was heart-wrenching. My Rakhi brother, Narinder, was visiting from London. The three of us drove up to Dehradun to drop him. When we reached the school, we met his Housemaster who was extremely warm and obviously used to handling situations like this one.

'Samrath, come with me. I'll introduce you to everyone.' When they came back, he said, 'Now say bye to your mother.' Sam looked at me and held out his hand to shake mine. 'Bye, Mamma.'

I took him in my arms and sobbed. He was trying hard not to break down. 'I'll be fine.'

Narinder caught my arm. 'Come on, Mira. We must go. Don't make it difficult for him.'

So I turned to leave. When I looked back one last time, I saw brave little Sam standing and waving, trying hard not to cry. I was inconsolable all the way to Delhi.

ST and I had been separated for two years by then. He sent me a note when he heard of Sam getting into school. 'Thank you for everything you have done. I have no worries now about my children.'

When he died a year later, not even forty years old, I grieved for the man he had been. So kind and warm and generous all his life, but at the end, there was no one around, none of the friends who had enjoyed his lavish hospitality.

It taught me a hard lesson about life.

10

What Is This Emotion?

It was June 1988 when I first met Brijesh. I knew of him. He was a close friend of Lalit Thapar and he knew my father as well. He had a reputation—there were rumours of his liaisons with charming women.

We met briefly in Delhi. He had dropped in with a friend of mine while I was in a tracksuit with oil in my hair. I said, 'Oh no!' when I saw someone walk in to visit.

He smiled, amused, and replied, 'Don't worry. You look fine.'

I was leaving for London in a few days. He said, 'You must call when you come,' and gave me his number.

In London, a week later, I was sharing a flat with a friend, Ritu Singh. Ritu was young, very attractive and very crazy! She loved doing things for shock value and it was her phase of wearing shorts and hats.

I was talking to her and I happened to take out Brijesh's number.

'He had asked me to call,' I told her.

'Of course you must,' Ritu said. 'What's he like?'

'Seemed nice, but I just met him for a bit and he might think it's too …'

'Rubbish! Call him.' And I made the call that changed my life.

We decided to meet that evening. He said, 'We can go for a drink to the Barracuda Club,' which was a very popular casino with a bar and restaurant.

I wore a black-and-white crêpe de Chine sari. It was a gift from my childhood friend Nina whom I loved, and it had been lucky for me every time I had worn it.

'Bye Miru …' Ritu said with wide eyes and a big smile. 'Wake me up when you come back and tell me all.'

'Don't be silly,' I said, 'I'm only going for a drink. I'll be back soon. Very soon. In an hour.'

He came to pick me up and we went to the club, where he seemed to know everyone.

'Do you come often?' I asked.

'Fairly often. I visit the casino.'

We sat at one of the small round tables and he bought the drinks—a malt whisky for him and a glass of wine for me. I was a little awkward in the beginning, but he was very disarming.

It seemed as if we had known each other for ages. He asked about my life, my marriage, my children, how much I missed my father. I was a fairly private person, but I found myself discussing everything with him.

Suddenly, the lights dimmed and there was a singer who came on the floor. I realized that it had been over two hours and it was almost ten p.m.

I said, 'It's very late, I must go. Ritu is waiting for me at home.'

He smiled and said, 'Actually, I didn't realize I would enjoy myself so much. I had a dinner that I'm now not going to. Let's dance. I'm sure she will understand.'

We danced. I couldn't remember when I had danced before. It was a haunting song.

Later, leading me to a table, he said, 'Come, let me get you some dinner or Ritu will get really angry!'

I can't remember what we ate. But we laughed and talked and talked. Finally, he dropped me home at about one a.m. I was in a daze. I thought to myself that I had never spent such a perfect evening with anyone before.

I had never felt like a beautiful woman the way I had felt with him. *Is this love?* I thought. *This must be what love feels like.*

I changed and got into bed. I thought, *Should I wake up Ritu? No ... talking about it might make the magic go away.* Finally, I slept.

When I got up the next morning, the phone was ringing.

'I haven't slept the whole night.' It was Brijesh. 'I have never felt this way before.'

That was the start. Nothing has been of more consequence ever. Nothing else has had that intensity.

I believe there is one person in the whole world who is made for you the same way that you are made for him or her. Your thoughts, the way you feel, are so attuned that you are one person.

He could feel my sadness, my joy, my apprehensions and would address everything before I could articulate them. There were many trips to London. His trips to India became frequent.

He became so much a part of my life that everything else was secondary.

But maybe so much happiness was probably not meant to be. God already had the whole plan ready.

It was December, the winter of 1989. Brijesh was catching the flight back to London. We had planned to go on a fishing trip, something he loved, with very close friends. His colleague and friend Helen Ward, an English girl who had become a good friend of mine, had come in a few days earlier.

He called me and said, 'I'm finishing a meeting. I'll go straight to the airport after that. See you tomorrow morning.'

'Don't miss the flight!' I told him.

That was the last time I spoke to him.

That night there was a call from London saying that Brijesh had had a heart attack on the meeting table. He was no more.

I have fragmented memories of that time. I rushed in the middle of the night next door to Jiti Mamu's.

'Call Brijesh, Jiti Mamu, someone is playing a joke.'

Jiti Mamu, Helen, my aunt, all of us kept calling. Each one finally got the news which we all knew but didn't want to accept. The doctor. Sedation. Complete devastation.

———

I remember other things from that period, as though time had frozen into a tableau.

Wanti, another childhood friend, was getting married at the time. Wanti's family and ours had known each other since our grandparents' generation. Her father, Uncle Inder, was adored by us all.

I was supposed to attend the wedding. I remember knowing that I would have to go. They were too close for me not to attend. I also remember how it felt, as though someone else was in my body. I strangely remember every single moment of that particular wedding.

And I remember the persistent deadness inside—as though someone had destroyed my soul.

There were some relationships forged during my time with Brijesh.

Anand Bahadur, who worked with Brijesh, became a dear friend. He was young, with a wonderful sense of humour. We tried out a series of disastrous matchmaking efforts for him, which thankfully didn't work, because he finally married a lovely girl. He was also quite shattered when Brijesh suddenly died.

Another one was Rahul Bajaj, an old friend of Brijesh's, whom I met very often during those days. As this book was about to go into print, I received the tragic news that Rahul is no more. Outspoken, disconcertingly frank and unsentimental, but always a good friend. I started tying a Rakhi on him thirty years ago, and until the end I received his customary box of Cadbury's chocolates every year.

I had asked him to suggest a lawyer during our talks with Estée Lauder. He immediately called Zia Mody, a prominent lawyer and someone he knew well, and asked her to meet with me.

When I called to thank him, he said tersely, 'Don't thank me. Just keep me updated.'

I will miss you, Rahul, and my Raksha Bandhans will not be the same again.

Gradually, you learn to live again. You have to. There is no choice.

I had no one to take care of my children, so I needed to work. I went to one of Brijesh's friends whom I knew and asked him for a job. He had a travel agency. I said I would take on whatever he thought I could do. He was fine with that and started me on client servicing. I had a nine-to-six job.

I would force myself to get up in the morning to go to work and come back tired in the evening. Mrs Simon—yes, she was still there—was her thoughtful self, with solace, serving nourishing soups and hot-water bottles, appearing with quiet consistency.

If she ever heard me crying behind closed doors, she never showed it but always remained comfortably reachable.

And that is how I think I got my life back into some semblance of order again. A large role in it was Mrs Simon's.

My father's death also devastated her—she told me much later, 'He was so kind to me, nobody has ever been so kind.' Yet, she was so busy looking after everyone in their cocoons of grief that her own misery seemed not even of any consequence to anyone.

She was with me when we shifted upstairs, she prayed to Jesus when we wanted a tenant and she made me go to sleep many times after the demons came when Brijesh died.

She looked after the children, both Sam and later Diviya as well. She fed them, helped with their studies, played games with them.

She was there through our most difficult times and made life easier.

Then one day, she got a call to say that her mother was very unwell and she had to go home.

I got her a train ticket. I remember thinking, 'I wish I had money,' because that day I desired nothing more than to be able to give her a good life. It was not to be.

Many years later, when things were different, I tried to track her down. I even took a flight to Madurai and went to all the churches to find out if they had a Mrs Simon in their congregation. But she had disappeared. I could never thank her or show her what she meant to me, to us. I could not do for her what I wanted to, what she so deserved. It was too late.

11

Rishikesh Appears

A few months after Brijesh died, the second major entity in my life arose into view—Rishikesh.

It strikes me often how Brijesh and Rishikesh, both pivots of my existence, became connected, and how this then led to Forest Essentials. I must go backwards in time to explain Rishikesh.

We had a property there, a private hunting lodge, which belonged to the Maharaja of Tehri Garhwal. He was a friend of my father. They were close hunting and fishing companions. On one of their trips together, my father had said to him that if he ever wanted to sell the property, my father would feel privileged to buy it. He would look after it the way the Maharaja himself would have done.

Due to some personal reasons, soon after that, the Maharaja indeed decided to sell the property and he told my father that he wanted him to have it.

We were in Madras in those days.

Once, when Papa was going up to Rishikesh after an Agreement to Sell had been signed, he invited Lalit Thapar to go with him. Lalit went, loved it and said to my father, 'Let's buy it together. We will both use it and enjoy it.' Papa couldn't refuse him.

So, it was bought in both their names.

Two years later, when my father died, there was no will. His only inheritors were my sister and myself. I had to go to the courts and put applications in both our names to get the properties of my father mutated, when I had never done anything like that in my life earlier.

Finally, when the paperwork was done, there were two properties. One where we lived in Delhi in Panchsheel Park and the other one in Rishikesh.

———

I had never visited the Rishikesh property but knew that Papa loved it. I asked Rajiv, the Chartered Accountant who looked after our affairs at the time, if he would come up with me to visit it. He said, as everyone else did, 'Sell it to Lalit Thapar. You have enough problems, how will you look after another property? There is no money or there's just about enough to take on what you have with the Panchsheel house.'

I said, 'Let's go and see it, Rajiv.'

'All right. If you really want to,' he said. He came with me.

I called Lalit and said, 'Lali Uncle, I want to go up to see the property. How do I go?'

He said that he would speak to the caretaker and I could get directions from his office. I was determined to go despite not getting clear directions on how to reach the property. We went. It was a fairly tortuous drive thirty years ago—no roads, no lights, no signs.

Anyway, we reached at about seven in the evening after leaving Delhi at five in the morning.

We drove in. The sun was setting. As we drove through the Rishikesh property gate, we caught a view of the Ganga!

Yes, the fabled Ganga river, flowing undisturbed along the land. The sheer magnitude of it made me catch my breath.

Then I saw the house. It was originally a hunting lodge—a beautiful old building, in beautifully polished teak wood and limestone.

We were to see later the perfectly preserved old wooden flooring and elegant staircases, high ceilings and stone fireplaces. Next to it stood its own ancient Shiv temple. And a perfect little cottage that the Maharaja had built for the acclaimed Guru Anandamayi Ma in perfect harmony with the setting. She had actually lived there for many years and worshipped at the temple. A litchi grove covered the land, sloping into its own pebble beach to touch the river, cradled by thick forests of hills on all sides.

Peace and beauty hung about like a cool haze over the scene.

What we were seeing could not be described. We were not prepared for the beauty of the place.

'I understand, Mira,' Rajiv said. 'Take your decision.' He knew what I would decide.

It was 1985. Lalit Thapar was the Chairman of Thapar Industries, a formidable giant. He wanted to retain Rishikesh, which was just one of the many properties that he had.

He offered to buy us out.

'Mira, Chander and I paid two lakhs to buy it. I'm going to be generous and give you double—four lakhs for just half. I do understand that you have an emotional bond with it, but you're welcome to come up whenever you want. You just have to call my office and they will arrange it.'

'Lali Uncle, I don't want to sell.'

Lalit looked taken aback. For a moment he was quiet.

Then he said, 'Are you crazy? What will you do with it? Do you even understand how these properties are maintained?'

I shook my head. *No.*

'I have a glass factory here that looks after the maintenance of Rishikesh. These places need a lot of constant inputs—huge financial inputs, Mira … I am telling you! Don't be ridiculous. Just take the money. I'm sure you'll get something reasonable around Delhi.'

It's not what he said that bothered me. I had known him since childhood. He used to visit us very often in Southend Lane and we used to go to his house with Papa and Mummy through the years.

It was his arrogance towards me. Had he said it differently, I might well have gone with him, because, yes, keeping it was a major decision in the situation I was in.

But when he was so dismissive, something snapped in me and I said, 'No, I will not sell.'

It was, of course, a difficult decision. I had the whole of the so-called Delhi society questioning what I was doing. 'She's challenging Lalit Thapar?', 'What does she think of herself?', 'Do you know that Chander had already sold it to Lalit?', 'Do you know that Lalit had put in all the money?', 'They had a pact that if one of them died it would go to the other and he's being so compassionate to the girls.'

I heard so very much, but I had made up my mind.

I then sent Lalit a letter saying that he could keep the Maharaja's house, the temple, the outhouses, everything—just give us half the land on the other side, where we could build.

I would never give up this property. It belonged to my father.

After all, it was he who had found it and bought it originally. And now Choti and I had inherited it after him.

Lalit would understand my decision. He had his share. We wanted to keep ours.

Jiti Mamu was furious: Choti's in-laws had asked for a divorce; she was in and out of rehabilitation which he and I were looking after, and there was no money available, so how were we going to take care of her expenses?

'How do you think you are going to build?' he said to me. 'You are also taking on someone whom you shouldn't make an enemy of.'

'Jiti Mamu, I don't care who he is. I don't want to sell.'

We argued. In the end, he said, 'Fine, you can be stubborn and do what you want.'

Finally, Lalit did get Choti's share because she had to sell part of it to him, much against my wishes, for her rapidly growing doctor's expenses, but that is how it was.

The choice was either selling her share of Rishikesh or of Panchsheel Park. It was interesting that half her share went to him and half to his lawyer, who was willing to pay a higher price and also was the only one who could take on Lalit by offering to buy her share. So eventually, against his wishes, Lalit Thapar also paid a higher price than he wanted to.

Now it was the year 1990.

I contacted the Bank Manager who had given me the previous loan and explained what I wanted to build in Rishikesh. 'What will you do with it?' he asked. 'It seems to be in the wilderness.'

'The area is beautiful; I will rent it out to someone as a guest house.'

I asked for the bare minimum loan and gave him the house papers, which had been just retrieved earlier.

I decided to go up to Rishikesh. I took the money I received with me. My daughter, Diviya, was back from Madras by then. My niece, Sagarika, must have been about five years old. I took both of them with me.

We went up to the Maharaja's old house, where, by now, I was not allowed to stay by Lalit Thapar. So we stayed in the outhouse above the servants' quarters. The staff very kindly took it upon themselves to allow us this since some were servants of Lalit's whom I had known since childhood.

We settled into our surroundings. The day was drawing to a close.

We had a mad evening. I actually took out all the money I had. I divided it like we were playing a game.

'Okay, Diviya,' I said, handing her a few bundles, 'get yourself a plane.' My face was flushed. My voice was almost hysterical, but this was fun.

'No, Mamma, I'm getting us a big-big house with lots of big-big gardens.' Diviya was looking at me with her solemn eyes, giggling as well now. She knew my fascination for gardens.

Shagu said in an excited, breathless voice, 'I want to get ... many many chocolates.' And she looked far away at imaginary chocolate mountains.

So we played with great abandon using the money for whatever we could imagine. After some time, I said to the children, 'Now put the money away because I don't know when we will see so much money again. We have to save it. It has to go to build Bara Papa's house here in Rishikesh.'

Envisaging the house and the building of it was more of a Herculean task than I had realized! Obviously, we couldn't afford an architect, so I had brought up a magazine that I had found some years earlier and kept carefully. There was a picture in it of the front and back of a beautiful home in the English countryside. This was what the house should look like!

In those days, labour in Uttaranchal was virtually non-existent. But there were those who built their own houses in the villages. Through our local caretaker of the house, I called in some labourers and showed them the picture.

They were stumped. They could not imagine what it was or how to go about building such a structure. The Thekedar, or contractor, dismissively said, '*Yeh hai kya? Yeh ghar hai?*' in disbelief.

Somehow, I started the building of the house. Water was brought in buckets from the river. Bricks and cement were brought up slowly in small trucks as the roads could not accommodate larger ones. There were no building plans. No drawings for plumbing or electricity. It just went on organically. 'Oh my God, we need a door here', 'Don't you think this room looks too large? We should make it into two.'

I now ask myself sometimes, 'How on earth did it happen? All of it?' And I don't know.

There was one more thing. I had antagonized Lali Uncle. After the first visit, Lalit said that the main house was not available, and I could not stay there. So I used to drive up to Rishikesh three times a week with Moti Lal, my trusted old driver, for eight to nine hours, reach at twelve or one p.m., spend four hours there and leave at four in the afternoon to get home at one or two a.m. This continued twice a week for almost six months and then once a week for another year.

I never requested Lalit to let me stay in the main house, which was still partly ours by right.

However, I sometimes spent the night in the outhouse, furnished with a rickety bed and one chair and table. There was also a fan that moved very slowly. So, in summer it was very hot in that room. Winters were freezing so we would carry extra blankets in the car.

'It's an adventure,' I used to tell the children whenever they came up with me.

'Can't we have some other kind of adventure?' my little Diviya would say.

'It will get more exciting as we go along, beta.'

———

Lalit Thapar was actually quite instrumental in my journey towards courage and determination. He cut off the water and electricity when I started building and this made me determined to get my own water and electricity.

I began by asking around about how I could apply for these. I was told that it could only be done from Lucknow, from the State Government offices, and got the address.

So, one day, my driver and I drove to Lucknow from Delhi to get the electricity connection. When we reached, the Chowkidar wanted to know whom we had come to meet. I said I couldn't remember his name but he was waiting for me. Maybe my desperation looked genuine, and he let us through.

It turned out to be a series of visits to find the right official. I finally met one official who first looked at me incredulously and then asked me the reason for the visit.

He looked at me and said, 'Come tomorrow. It is our closing time.'

I think I had had it after my trip and the long wait, and I started crying. He was an elderly man and looked shocked.

'Okay, okay, beta, what is it?'

He stayed on for almost two hours more, asked for papers and then called for files.

'Hmm … this already has electricity. It is the Maharaja's property.' I told him all the facts, coming to the part where the electricity had been cut off. Finally he handed over a paper and said, 'Your electricity has been restored. Now you should apply for a separate connection.'

It happened without any bribes or any payout.

I continued to build. It was sporadic and slow. Many times, I had to stop because there was no money.

In the meantime, the water problem was becoming overwhelming. I was told that if I needed a water connection, I would again have to go to the Government Headquarters in Lucknow. We couldn't do much without water—the old litchi and mango trees would dry up and it was increasingly difficult to get buckets from the river.

So, Lucknow it was again. I stayed with some friends who lived there and went to the relevant government offices. It was a huge campus with beautiful buildings, all bureaucratic offices. They were like a maze. It took four days to figure out who the right person was and also quite a lot of dexterity to get him at his table between the tea breaks!

His name was Mr Chakraborty and he was the Head of the Forest Division. His desk was overflowing with books and files and documents—I couldn't understand how he could look at anything. Anyway, he was quite surprised to get a visitor like me and asked what I wanted.

'Bhaisaab,' I said, 'only you can help me. My trees are dying. I'm making a house and my water connection is cut, so there's no water.'

He stopped what he was doing and said, '*Poori baat batao!*'

I told him the whole story. He wanted to know all the details. '*Paani kisne kaata?*'

When I said 'Thapar', he knew of him.

He listened keenly, especially the parts where the water and
electricity had been cut off. He said, '*Umar to aapki kum hai par himmat
hai.*' Though he didn't look like it, he was surprisingly clued in. He
took out a map from somewhere and said, 'This is the nearest water
source. This is forest land, but I am going to give you a connection
so the pipe can go over it.' He marked out a path in red ink, called
someone and gave him directions, saying 'Take down her full name
and the address at Gular Dogi.'

'You will get a lease on the water and have to pay a yearly fee of Rs
600. Water will be available immediately. Your trees will not die. *Khush
hain aap?*' He saw my face. 'Good. *Jaiye.*'

That was it. We had the water that we desperately required.

12

Karan Singh

On one of our trips, Diviya and Sagarika had driven up with me. Since it had taken longer to leave, we reached quite late.

It was not safe to drive that late in the hills, so I decided that we would spend the night in the outhouse again. The cook there was sympathetic and insisted on rustling up some eggs for the children and me. We ate and went upstairs.

At the time, there used to be a new caretaker at the property, called Karan Singh.

He was retired from the army and was an aggressive personality. He seemed about seven feet tall, with a luxuriant moustache and a booming voice. He fancied himself to be Lalit's right-hand man and was antagonistic to me, although only covertly till then. He carried a gun. Everyone in the area was terrified of him. He did not like the idea that we had been fed in the kitchen. I heard him scolding the cook, 'I will tell Saab what you are doing ...'

This was in November and it was cold in Rishikesh. The children and I got into bed, one child on either side of me. The lights were off. We were sleeping. Suddenly, I heard a banging on the door. I got up and looked at my watch—it was midnight.

'Who is it?'

'You people better come out and I will show you what I can do.'

It was Karan Singh, and he was drunk. The door was shaking. I had locked it with the latch. But it was unsteady and would not last long. Shaking with fear, I got the chair lying near the bed and wedged it against the door to prevent it from opening.

The children had got up and were now crying.

'Open up!' He was now banging on the door.

I made the children stay put on the bed and said, 'Now say your prayers, "Ik Onkar Satnam".'

Both the girls closed their eyes and began repeating the prayer. We sat huddled on the bed for what seemed like hours, shivering and frightened. Finally, he went away.

We heard him cursing and going down the stairs. The children went to sleep.

I was awake the whole night.

Early next morning, I went down and called my driver, Moti Lal. I told him what had happened the night before. We went together to the site where the labourers had gathered for the construction work.

I told them to start work. After about an hour, we heard someone behind us. It was Karan Singh.

'Stop the work,' he said.

'The work will not stop,' I replied.

I remember thinking, *Where am I getting the courage to do this?*

The workers did not know what to do—some started working and some stopped in fear.

I stood there with the children clinging to me. Moti, all five feet of him, thin and gnarled, had found a stick from somewhere and was brandishing it in front of the monstruous man who didn't even bother to look at him.

He was looking at me. Then he took out his gun and held it to my head. The children started kicking him and crying.

'Leave my Masi alone,' Shagu sobbed.

'Mamma, what is he doing? Stop it you …' Diviya was shaking with fear and anger.

I just snapped. I could feel my temperature rising. I pushed Karan Singh's hand away and shoved both the children in the car.

'*Moti, chalo.*' We had to act.

'*Main isko maar doonga.*' Moti was unstoppable suddenly.

'No, let's go.'

We left the house, I in my mud-splattered cotton salwar-kameez and voluminous mulmul dupatta, grubby from the hands of the children and my own cold sweat-stained hands.

We drove down to Rishikesh town for the first time. It was a picturesque little local town.

'Let us find the police station,' I said to Moti. After asking for directions, we drove to the only police station in town. There was no one at the desk.

I said, 'I want to put in a complaint,' to some bewildered person who came in.

'Complaint?'

'Is there anyone I can talk to?'

Eventually, after much back and forth, they said they had called the new police officer. We waited patiently in the police station.

Someone came in. He was young and seemed courteous.

'Can I help you?' It was the new officer.

'Yes. I am here to put in a complaint about Karan Singh, the caretaker of the Thapar House. He attempted to attack me last night and again today. I want to file a complaint against him.'

When he heard 'Thapar House', he became cautious, since no one wanted to upset the owner of the house. It was pretty much a Lord-of-the-Manor approach there, it seemed.

'What happened?'

I explained in great detail about Karan Singh's behaviour the previous night and earlier during the day.

'He put a gun to Masi's head and said "I will shoot",' said my five-year-old niece, who always had a flair for drama. 'I will shoot him if he comes near her.'

I think he understood the situation. He was new to the area and its complications.

I appealed to him to get the police to stop Karan Singh, as otherwise how could anyone ask for justice? He heard me out and then said, 'Don't worry. I will take your complaint, Thapars or no Thapars. There is right and justice in our country. This is why we are there.'

I wrote the complaint, and I am told that Karan Singh was arrested by the police within four hours.

We left Rishikesh and drove straight to Delhi. We stopped nowhere to eat and were in an emotional state, where no one spoke much.

The children were quiet, Moti was angry and I was burning with fever and livid with anger.

We reached Delhi at about ten p.m. and I said to Moti, 'Please drive straight to Lalit Thapar's home on Ratendone Road.'

He was surprised but said nothing and drove there. We went in and parked. I told the children to wait and went inside.

The door was opened by one of the old servants whom I knew well. I asked for Lalit and he asked me to come in. In retrospect, I must have looked very strange in the state I was in. Dishevelled, flushed and with an almost 103-degree temperature. He said Saab had some guests and he would call him.

Lalit was entertaining and there seemed to be a party on. He saw me and came out. 'How are you, Mira? Where are you coming from? Come in.'

I had no idea any longer of the niceties of how I should say things and I just broke down.

It was not important to me who was there or not.

I was hysterical.

'You have allowed your man Karan Singh in Rishikesh to threaten me and my children. He has held a gun to my head. There is no way he could have done that without your approval. For what? Because I don't want to sell my property? I will not. I don't care how you threaten me.'

He said, 'Mira, calm down, you are very upset. I don't know what you are talking about.'

I said 'I have come straight from there to tell you this. I am going back home now. You need to do whatever you think is right.'

I did see that many of his guests were most intrigued by our conversation and listening in. They were of no interest to me. Most were the biggest sycophants anyway. I left.

Later I learnt that Karan Singh was brought down by the police and shifted from the position he had in Rishikesh to one of the other Thapar factories.

We never saw him again.

———

Many years later, after I had built the Rishikesh property, Lalit dropped in one New Year's Eve. I was surprised to see him. I called him in for a drink. He accepted.

'Chander would have been very proud of you,' he said. 'Didn't think you would do it.'

That was enough. It put everything to rest.

13

Life's Learnings Continue

I often wonder how I coped in those years; I think I had possibly no time to feel sorry for myself. There was too much to be done. The house in Panchsheel, educating the children, Choti, fighting for Rishikesh and trying to keep myself from going under. Life continued.

Diviya had now settled down with me in Panchsheel. ST had passed away.

The Rishikesh property had been let out to a bank. It took care of immediate daily expenses.

As for Choti, she had just returned from her convalescence. The doctor suggested that I should find something interesting for her to do.

A friend of mine, P.J. Singh, ran an advertising agency. I spoke to him and explained the situation. PJ was very nice about it. He agreed to let Choti work in the agency for a stipend. It would be interesting for her to learn as she went along. He also suggested to his staff that they needed to be protective about her.

Everything seemed to be going fine. But about a month later, she seemed to be developing a friendship in the office. The man, Krishna Prasad, was a South Indian. Though he seemed to be very friendly with Choti, he explained to PJ that it was just platonic; she was a very nice but misunderstood person and that was all.

Slowly, I stumbled upon the realization that she had begun to go to Krishna Prasad's house, pretending to be in the office. PJ confronted him with this information, but he still insisted that it was all above board.

One day, we discovered that they had run off together. They got married and came back to me after that. They said they had thought about it and decided it was best for them both. Choti said that she had never been happier. I was completely shocked.

'But Choti, how can you do this! Don't you need to be well first? You're not okay. Get okay first before you complicate your life!'

But there was nothing to do except to give in. They were at Panchsheel now, asking for my blessings.

In the meantime, PJ asked Krishna Prasad to leave, saying that he had let PJ down and that he would find it difficult to trust Krishna Prasad again. Krishna Prasad and Choti moved to a barsati where he lived at the time.

After a few months, Krishna Prasad called me. 'She is not well again.'

'What can I say, Krishna Prasad ... what else were you expecting!'

Jiti Mamu and I were back to visiting the doctors again.

It was many years later, after Choti came out of this state and found herself pregnant once again and had her son Jai, that she got into another world of pandits, astrologers and visiting temples.

———

At home, Sam was preparing to leave for the US for his studies. I did try to explain to him many times that we could not afford the US. It was not just the fees, everything else was not even factored in. However, he was overwhelmingly certain that this was what he wanted to do. Finally, after many preparations and overcoming many obstacles, Sam left for college.

There was no chance that I could accompany him to university to help him familiarize. I saw many parents who were able to go and make arrangements for staying and acclimatizing the child. There were absolutely no funds that allowed for that. Sam went alone and settled down without any support system. He must have often faced fear and uncertainty. He must have made mistakes. I often wondered how he would survive, managing in new surroundings, handling the budget which was always tight.

He certainly had less money than most of the other Indian students whom he knew from school or childhood. American children were brought up to fend for themselves, so they were much better equipped. It was very difficult to choose the right subjects and work out a career plan alone at eighteen, and inevitably many wrong choices were made. It was the way it was ... there were too many circumstances beyond one's control.

All I remember is that Sam never complained.

14

Candles and More Candles

It was the summer of 1999. We were spending a week in a cottage in the picturesque Ramgarh on a family holiday. The lights kept going off.

There were some candles in the room—always in short supply, so one day, I gathered all the melted-down candles and heated them in a pan. With the children, it was a project. There was a Coke can which was cut open by an industrious mali for me.

The wax was poured into the can with the leftover wicks. It lit! We were all thrilled. When I think back, that was probably the start of Candlemania.

My vision was for candles that were a delight to behold, made with real beeswax and giving out the fragrance of flowers and herbs, that would burn gently for hours. Only *that* to me was a candle. Nothing else was. And I intended to create that.

It seemed easy—melt the wax, mix in pure fragrant extracted oils, add a wick and bring it all together in a beautiful shape.

But first, the wax—what was available was mostly paraffin wax. Wicks were untreated cotton wicks that used to smoke. It seemed natural for me for essential oils to be in the wax for releasing real fragrance when a candle was lit. But it was difficult to find pure essential oils. Only synthetic scents were available for this.

When I tried to source actual beeswax, there was a problem. Then it struck me that beeswax would be found in villages. I discovered that in the villages, they would extract the honey from a honeycomb and pay no attention to the leftover beeswax. I tried to have this beeswax collected through local women and children. This would generate some employment and benefit them too.

But I found that a consistent supply was hard to come by. It needed perseverance.

By now, my head was full of candles. I could just see the candles I would make in the future—their myriad, beautiful, unique shapes. I could smell wood, leaf, flower, bark, fruit. One day, I sat myself down and thought soberly about what was happening. It was a love affair with an idea, yes, but I told myself that I also needed something to do.

That something should (and could!) make some money. Why not give candles a commercial try?

The millennium was ending. The year 2000 was approaching. A symbol of new beginnings.

I loved to travel. I began to collect candle moulds, wax, containers, colours, wicks, oils, to-do books, manuals. These now occupied the available spaces at home. The candles of my imagination gradually began to form for real—with the search for raw material and with experimenting.

Real candles became ready. And then more. And then many more. With pressed flowers, tree bark, in mother-of-pearl shell, with mirrors, in a gold look, in an antique silver look. Finally, I had an entire collection. It needed a name.

The name was sitting neatly in my mind, waiting its turn. I said it aloud: 'Candlemania.'

Yes, it was the beginning of mania. The magic, the mania—these still drive me.

At the end of 2000 I had a small exhibition in the house.

I called my cousin Vikram. 'Vicky, help me arrange everything.' He laid it out. Vicky, the little boy of years ago who had so dutifully drunk my 'American' milk-and-Coke out of loyalty to the 'Fantabulous Four', was now a gifted architect.

I invited everyone. 'I have been making candles out of beeswax and pure fragrant oils. My exhibition is at home … if you'd like to take a look, come over.' Exhibiting was not my forte. I only enjoyed the back-end work—to create. Anything else was a different matter.

As the day approached, I was very nervous. 'What if no one arrives?'

I had hired two boys to help me. But I had put my own hands to each step. Everything, from reading the books to mixing the colours to decorating the candles. With their help. And Diviya's. She had volunteered to help me out. Each time a candle finally emerged from the effort, I would compare it with the prototype in my head. Then all of us would look at the candle.

'Wow!'

'So nice!'

'*Bahut accha.*'

Then we would go for the next one.

The night before the exhibition I got a horrible thought: 'What if … what if, maybe, it is only just we who think these candles are great? What if no one wants them?'

Then another horrible thought: 'Who really loves me enough to buy the candles even if they hate them?'

Then I thought, no one possibly could. Luckily it was too late, so the exhibition took place.

It started.

The scene, filled with beauty, with fragrance, had the dread of a battlefront for me. A few people started trickling in. I had a forced smile and a calm outward demeanour. Empty drawing room. I shrank inside.

Then, like a wound-up toy unwinding, first slowly and then with increasing speed, the evening began to whir. A lot of people I knew came. And many I didn't know too! They bought candles. More people, more talk, more sales, more packing, more pleasant chatter, more bills.

It wasn't just the four of us who thought they were beautiful after all! Someone said, 'Miru, make a collection for retail.'

The evening passed in a pleasantly perfumed, crowded blur. After a while, I went into my bedroom and sat down to compose myself. We had started at four in the evening and by eight it was over. The candles had finished. We sold every one of them and many wanted to order more.

I had made one lakh that day. I couldn't believe it! It was the first time I had ever really earned money myself. I was so used to believing myself to be dependent on others. Even when I was trying to put my life together, I never thought I was doing anything exceptional.

I thought I was doing what anyone would have done in my place. Strong? Independent? Could that be me? I could have flown all the way up like a bright balloon that day.

15

Going to America

Almost a year had gone by since Sam had left for America. I missed him. It was a time when you could speak on the phone sporadically since there were no mobiles, but there were too many gaps between calls to actually be in touch on a consistent basis. Sam had always been such an integral part of my life that I wanted to share any small thing that happened with him, but he was not there.

I could still feel in his voice, every time I spoke with him, that there were some things he wanted to say but could not or did not—maybe because he did not want to put an additional burden on me. Many nights, I could not sleep imagining what he would be facing but there was nothing I could do.

Then one day, I remember it clearly, I got a call from America. I learnt that Sam was in hospital and was unable to move his right arm. The nameless caller assured me he was stable and under doctors' care. 'What did you say?' I heard myself scream. 'Why is his arm not moving? What is the problem?' The person at the other end was polite but perfunctory and said they currently had no other information.

I desperately tried to get through to the doctors, to the college, to his friends—but there was no clear information.

It was evening in India. I called Diviya who was in the next room. 'Diviya, your brother is not well, so we both have to go to him.'

She was in the middle of something and did not quite understand what I was saying. 'What has happened? Why are you crying, Mom? What has happened to Bhaiya?' I had no answers to give but my mind was in overdrive. I knew I could not have travelled alone in my state of mind, so Diviya and I needed to go together.

We both had passports but no visas for the US. I rang a dear friend, Harishankar Singhania, who I knew was a close friend of the American Ambassador. 'I need a favour,' I said, which is something I never normally did.

'Tell me, Mira. Why are you sounding so agitated? What can I do?' he said.

'Sam is in hospital in Rochester, and Diviya and I have no visas. I want to leave immediately. Please see what you can do.'

'Let me get back to you,' he said quietly. An hour later, he called and said he would have our passports collected that night and the visas would be stamped the next morning.

I don't know how we got through that night but we had tickets booked for the next night to leave for New York. It was a cramped, overcrowded flight and we both slept intermittently while I kept repeating the same prayer in my mind. Finally, we reached JFK, from where we were to take a connecting flight.

'Is this the plane?' It was a small one-propeller plane which looked like it had seen better days! *Oh God, please don't let us die before we can reach him*, I thought.

We both got into the aircraft, which took off and then shook violently from side to side through the entire duration of the flight. By the time we reached the airstrip in Rochester, we had been through a virtual whirlpool. Unsteadily, we both got off the aircraft.

While we were collecting our bags, there was a loud, 'Hi Mira Aunty, how are you? Hi Diviya. I've come to pick you up.' It was Rahul Munjal, a school friend of Sam who was also in college there, and whom we were delighted to see. He was in a bright Hawaiian shirt. He also had, as I was to discover later, an even brighter convertible in which he safely dropped us at the apartment that had been booked for us. He kept answering questions about Sam as best he could, which we inundated him with. 'I can take you to the hospital later once you settle in, Aunty,' he said. We just deposited our bags and requested him to take us there immediately, which he very kindly did.

The hospital was a maze. It was large and bright and white, and had green-coated doctors and nurses, all briskly involved in their own activities. I managed to get hold of a doctor and tried to explain what we had come for, but he was busy and said I would need to wait. Finally, he must have noticed my desperation and came back. 'Yes? How can I help?' he asked. I told him as concisely as I could about why we were there. 'Name? College?' He spoke to someone, came back and led us to a ward where there was a row of beds.

I saw Sam immediately. He was asleep with his arm resting on the blanket. Tears streaming down my cheeks, I waited for him to get up. Sometime later—and by now I had lost all track of time—he opened his eyes. 'Mom?' he said, smiled and went back to sleep.

His condition improved in the next few days and sensation slowly started returning to his arm. The doctor, who was quite friendly by now, said, 'Your prayers seem to have worked.' We were able to take him back to the apartment but had to bring him every day to the hospital to get physiotherapy for the next ten days.

The first two days, the three of us went. We had to pass a large shopping complex on the way, and I thought that it might be a good idea to drop Diviya there and pick her up on the way back.

'You can do some window shopping and look around—better than the hospital,' I told her.

So, we used to drop her off every day, with an assigned place to pick her up after two hours of physiotherapy. Things were fine until about the last day. We stopped to pick her up, but she didn't seem to be there. She was generally very punctual—maybe she had forgotten the time. We waited, fifteen minutes passed, half an hour and then an hour. By now, we were seriously panicking. We went everywhere possible, to all the stores she may have visited, but there was no sight of her. I could not believe this was happening—maybe someone had kidnapped her? Wild thoughts entered my mind. *What could have happened? Was she okay?*

Sam was tired and his arm was hurting. He was worried and anxious, and I was almost in a state of hysteria. The shops had started closing so we went to the help desk and gave her name to be announced, but there was no response. Finally, they took down our address and said they would let us know as soon as they had any news.

We went back to the apartment in a grey daze of misery. I had thought things could not have gotten worse than they already were. We just looked at each other and there was nothing to say.

Around ten p.m., suddenly, there was a knock on the door. I went to answer it and there were two policemen with Diviya in the centre. She had streaks of tears down her cheeks and looked terrified.

'Is this your daughter?' one of the policemen asked.

'Yes.' I nodded. Apparently, she had had a stomach ache and gone into a pharmacy, where they had given her some medication and asked her to sit down as she was in pain. She had fallen asleep in a chair at the back of this shop. They'd noticed her when they were closing and had informed the authorities.

The policemen were very sympathetic and said, 'That must have been a bad shock, lady. We are glad she is back safely.'

We thanked them profusely and then when they left, I caught hold of her and shook her. 'How could you do this to me?'

'I'm sorry, Ma, I just fell asleep.' She was crying.

It had been the most debilitating experience, the whole sequence, since the time we landed.

Exhausted, the three of us just hugged each other and cried and cried.

As I said to Sam much later, it was a suitably dramatic ending to the whole American episode.

16

Raju

When I was going to Lucknow quite frequently to meet with the authorities for all our water issues in Rishikesh, I used to stay with Rocky and Rekha Mohan, who owned the Mohan Meakin distilleries and were warm and hospitable hosts.

I met Raju Kulkarni and Somesh Kapai there, who were both involved in some work with Rocky at the time. We used to meet quite often and I found myself relaxing with them—Raju with his simplicity and Somesh with his wacky sense of humour.

It was still a time when I was so emotionally fragile that I thought I needed someone in my life to depend on. Raju increasingly became that person. He was straightforward and unflinchingly honest. To tell the truth, he and I were totally different people from different backgrounds and different worlds.

Maybe the fact that I had not really met someone like him before was quite refreshing for me. When he tentatively proposed, I accepted—I am not sure whether he was more surprised or I! As impetuous as ever, I did not stop to think of the larger implications. I had obviously not yet come to that stage in my life where I was confident of my abilities, and still thought I was dependent.

Many people I knew closely said that I should reconsider as there was no meeting ground between the two of us, but I chose to go ahead. I think our lives together for those few years were a blur. It was a time of great change. Diviya's marriage, Sam going to college in the US, and my need to do something.

It was evident that we were not compatible, increasingly so, and perhaps inevitably so.

Soon after, we decided it was best to live separately. It was the only thing to do. However, it did teach me one thing. We define ourselves with the kind of people we think we are, and sometimes those boundaries are so clear that we don't go beyond them. However, out of all this emerged an unlikely friendship which we both cherish.

The most amazing thing is that his family has, over the years, become fairly integrated with my family and my children and the grandchildren love him dearly, as he does them.

For him, our priorities come before his own.

Most of the time, we judge others by conventional standards. Courageous was not a word I associated with Raju, but when I saw him battling cancer quietly much later, standing by his family according to his beliefs, or when it came to honouring commitments that most people would not do, I realized it is part of who he is.

17

Pure Indulgence

I was very keen that Diviya should study, that she should have a professional life in whichever field she was passionate about. I tried to send her in that direction. But she would always say the same thing.

'No, Mamma, I want a home and children.'

'Diviya, you can have that anyway ...'

'I love families, Mom.'

When she was a little over twenty-one, she began seeing Hitesh, her future husband.

Today she may want her own individuality, her self-expression. But back then, she wanted different things. In spite of my best efforts for Diviya to be an independent woman, she wanted domesticity and belonging. Hitesh's parents approached me. They were traditional. It was a conservative Punjabi family, with a background very different from ours.

I was concerned. But Diviya seemed to want it all. The big joint family, the giving and the taking and all the rituals and more of large conservative Punjabi families.

I was broke. How was I going to fulfil the requirements of this wedding?

I still marvel at how miraculously resources organically appeared at the time, just right for the wedding. One day, a friend came and handed me an envelope that eventually helped cover some wedding expenses. He knew that Diviya's wedding was on, but I had not even remotely expected what was coming. Long ago, I had introduced him to another friend whom he had wanted to meet. I had no idea why and neither did I ask.

'You remember that favour you had done me years ago?'

'Which favour?' I said, a little puzzled.

'Remember when you introduced me to your friend? Well, my business deal went through at that time and I have not looked back since.'

'I know. I'm so glad. That was lucky.'

Then he put an envelope next to me and said, 'I just wanted to say thanks.'

'Oh no.' I returned the envelope. 'This isn't called for at all.'

'But Mira, you must understand that I would happily have given it to anyone who had made the introduction. So why not you? You also may require it at this time.'

He must have known. I had no answer. A miracle had occurred.

Diviya never asked for anything. She only had her heart set on a gold-and-white Rohit Bal outfit which she knew we could not afford.

I tried to figure out how we could buy it but to my despair, it was not possible. One of my friends said that something similar could be made. So we decided to go with that instead. And finally, Diviya got her gold-and-white wish fulfilled, not as I would have wished, but it would have to make do. It cost a lot less than the Rohit Bal one. I vowed to get her that when I could afford it.

After Diviya got married, I began to see her as a family unit and not as Diviya, the person. She was part of a unit comprising Hitesh, her children, her whole family. Diviya had wanted the safety and security of a large joint family controlled by tradition and she had fit right in.

Perhaps it was an unlived part of her personality. Then came several years where she was so much a part of her extended family that our interactions became much less.

Today, Diviya wants to be someone in her own right. Maybe it took all that before she could eventually come to this point.

———

Some months after Diviya's wedding, however, something happened which created a life-changing shift for me. It seemed innocuous at the time.

I moved slowly from candle-making to making soap. Life-changing, because it would be much more than just soap. It would be the birth of Forest Essentials. Although I had no idea at the time.

The candle orders continued to come. To cope with them, my garage was now also my little office. The two boys had become three. A little shed was made for them behind the garage. I realized I needed some more people to help me. I must have mentioned this to my Chartered Accountant, Rajiv.

Sometime later, he said, 'I have someone who is an Accountant. She is a lady and maybe you can use her part-time.'

She came to see me. She was a small South Indian lady called Malathi.

'I can help with accounts and bookkeeping,' she said, 'but I can only come for half a day three times a week.'

That was fine. I had discussed her salary with Rajiv.

'I can pay you Rs 3,000 a month, if that's okay?'

'That's okay,' she said.

Things progressed. There were more orders. The business was getting better. I needed more help. I then interviewed and employed a girl, Ritu. She was bright and smart.

If I am asked to sum up what those days felt like in a word, it was actually fun.

———

That year, I had gone to meet Sam in Rochester. On my way, in New York, I attended a Quaker class for handmade soap. I was very intrigued. They had various ingredients, all natural, and there was a certain method to mixing and incorporating the ingredients at specific times in the process and finally pouring it into a mould to make a slab of soap. I loved it. The knowledge, the science, the creation, the beauty, the practical use and the actual physical end result in your hands.

Soon, the idea of soap began to take a clearer shape—why didn't we have good quality soaps in India? Rishikesh, ancient and steeped in tradition, was the home of Ayurveda, which, I was convinced, did have recipes for soap. An Ayurvedic soap would have the qualities that I was chasing. In Rishikesh, I went to see how these soaps were being made.

The method was similar to what I had learnt in the Quaker class. But the ingredients were substandard, just like I had seen with candles. It did not match my vision of what a soap should look like, or feel like. The lack of high-quality ingredients was reflected in the soaps themselves. This lack of quality intrigued me. I wanted to make a superior soap happen. It was possible.

The knowledge was there. I tracked down some Ayurvedic Vaids to ask about more formulations for soaps. All the formulations suggested pure, fresh, cold-pressed oils. Nothing of the kind was being used.

It was a curious situation. We had the most amazing traditional formulations. Soaps were being made using those formulations, with the help of Vaids, by large companies that concentrated on Ayurvedic products. But the ingredients were not what was prescribed. Procuring those high-quality ingredients was very expensive. No one would buy an expensive end product—a simple soap.

There was a wall. It was visible—a soap is an ordinary utility that everyone uses. Its saleability would vanish if we used high-quality raw material, which would make the cost too high. Also, most Ayurvedic formulations required that the product be cured for weeks before it was matured and made ready for use. All this added to the selling price.

I collected more books; I had recipes translated from the original Sanskrit transcripts; I met manufacturers of Ayurvedic soaps.

Each time I faced the same obstacle.

But as I saw it, expensive or not, there was no other way that they should be.

I could see only those products. Ayurveda intended nothing less. For me, they needed to be created.

There was an advantage to the higher price: I had the surety of an excellent, pure product. Middle- and upper-class users could afford it and probably would want such a product if it were available. I was convinced that a high-quality product would work regardless of cost.

How was I to convey to them the promise that if they used a fabulous soap, which was great for their skin, the more they used it, the more they would love it? I was sure they would be willing to pay the price for it if they understood.

As usual, the answer suddenly came to me. Our products must also look and feel pleasurable, taste delicious and smell divine. They should be enjoyable in every way. I needed to conjure up both together—effectivity and pleasure. Not just Ayurveda, but products which would be handmade to the most exacting specifications and could now be available off the shelf. That was true opulence!

Had no one seen it before? Is it possible that only I could see it? Traditional formulations for beautiful, health-giving products were lying with us for centuries, waiting to be used.

They just needed the elegance and purity that was missing.

Luxurious Ayurveda was our answer.

18

Hemant

I needed to make those soaps. I started trying to figure out the next steps.

I had no idea of how I should go about it.

I looked at my recipes. That's all I had. My recipes said to use oils: fresh, cold-pressed black sesame oil and pure coconut and almond oils. I started by asking at home, 'Where can I get pure, cold-pressed oils?'

My old cook said, 'Pure oils? For what? What are cold-pressed oils?'

'Cold-pressed means pressed from seeds, by hand, without heat.'

I thought my household staff would know. What did they do in their villages?

I was explained to, gently, that everything in the market was adulterated. It was only in the village that people would take out oil by hand in small amounts to use for themselves. To sell pure oil was too expensive. Everyone took this fact as a matter of course. 'Otherwise, who will buy it?'

'At home, in the village, we take out oil for our own needs from our own seeds from our land, using a kolhu. But here, in a city, we have to buy it.

'We buy mustard oil at Rs 70. If you were to buy mustard oil made like that from mustard seeds, it would cost much more. Who would buy it?'

I could not believe that an oil that was completely fresh and pure was out of my reach unless we hand-pressed it ourselves.

But it was true. I then thought backwards—there must be some manufacturers of pure oil. They would stock it. They would make it available to wholesalers.

Since I was going to make soap, I would anyway need large quantities. To me, a large quantity was something like fifty litres.

So now I had to find a wholesaler of oils.

Where? The job was given to intrepid Chotu, my driver. He was Moti's son. Moti was old and had retired by now. Chotu found out that in Sadar Bazaar, a market in the bowels of Old Delhi, there were offices of wholesalers. One step forward …

'Okay, good,' I said. 'So Chotu, now you go there and see who can supply us oil.'

Chotu was usually sure of himself and comfortable in most situations. But he was a bit baffled by this.

'What oils shall I ask for?'

'Chotu, really! Ask for almond oil, olive oil, sesame oil. And, of course, see what else he has.'

So Chotu went to Sadar Bazaar. He asked a few people. He was directed to the offices of one of the oldest oil wholesale companies. Its board was prominently visible.

He went up to the first man inside. It turned out to be the proprietor's son, Hemant, who just happened to be there. He used to visit occasionally only to please his father and was not really interested in his father's business. Chotu had no idea of this, of course.

He went up to him and proceeded to ask for what he required. Hemant was to remember it very distinctly later. And was full of admiration for Chotu's spirit. Chotu, it seems, launched into some kind of incoherent version of what I had told him, but he did get the point across. He came to the crux of the matter with, 'I want to buy oil because my Memsaab wants to make soap. She wants oil with no adulteration.'

Hemant became very curious. No talk of price.

This was not the normal kind of buyer who strolled into their offices. He decided to warm up to Chotu because this was such an aberration from their usual buyer-and-seller routine.

'Who is your Memsaab? What soaps does she want to make?'

Chotu then decided that this was beyond him. He lifted up his hands, shrugged and took one step back. '*Aap unse hi baat kar lijiye.*' It was beyond his comprehension.

So, I got a call from Chotu. 'I have met someone from the wholesale oil company, his name is Hemant, please talk to him.' He handed the phone to Hemant.

'Hello ji,' said Hemant. 'How can I help you?'

'I want to give a large order for oil. But it has to be pure,' I said. 'I will take fifty litres.' I smiled to myself. The quantity seemed really impressive.

'Fifty litres?' Hemant repeated.

'Yes.'

I think, at first, he was incredulous. They were wholesalers who sold in tonnes. Then he was amused. And finally, he was quite curious.

'What do you need it for?'

'I want to make the best quality Ayurvedic soap,' I said.

'Actually, I also make soaps as my hobby sometimes,' he said. 'Can I come meet you? My name is Hemant.'

'Please do come, Hemantji. Chotu will give you my address.'
We fixed to meet.

It was the first of many meetings. Later one day, Hemant confessed,
'I've only made washing soap, so I don't know how to make soap from
your ingredients, but I do have experience.'

Initially, Hemant took me to show how oil sourcing was being done
at present.

We went to little stores, tucked away in by-lanes in Sadar Bazaar,
where all kinds of scents were sold—from 'pure' coconut oil, to 'pure'
mustard oil to 'pure' almond oil.

You just had to add a few drops to even machine oil and it would
smell like the real thing!

'Not this kind of oil, Hemant. I want pure oil that is real. Fresh
herbs. Flower extracts. Essential oils.' It was a world that was alien to
him.

But over time, we had developed a camaraderie.

'Who can make soap from all these, ma'am? Who will buy them?'

'You don't worry about that! Tell me how to make almond oil,' I
said.

'From almonds. If you want real almond oil.' I learnt to buy raw
material.

Hemant took me to buy almonds. He was shaking his head. Was he
not getting through to me?

'There are people who will buy them, Hemant. And there are people
who want to use what is good for them. It's just that it's not available.
I'm going to make them and people will want to buy.'

'Who will believe they are very pure and made in the Ayurvedic
way, ma'am?' Hemant always called me 'ma'am'.

'Once they see it, once they try it on themselves. They will know
the difference.'

Of course, Chotu was there on the sidelines.

He prophesized, '*Kabhi nahi chalega, madam. Yeh to khali gaon mein
hum karte hain, apne liye.*' He was sure this project was off to a wrong
start, that only villagers used oil which they had to extract from their

own produce. Why would someone bother to pay for this if they could buy a ready-made branded product like the ones already existing in the market? Who would check to see how pure this new thing was?

Anyway, I wanted to make this soap. So, everything between me and making such a soap had to be cleared away.

'My soap' was to be made with the best ingredients. None of the soaps in the market cost more than fifteen to twenty rupees.

It was simple. If there were buyers for my soaps that would be wonderful. If there were not many people who wanted what I thought was worth having, then it would remain an enjoyable hobby. So, at the very least, it would channel my creative energy, my time and my focus.

Every day, I kept repeating the basic soap-making process, fine-tuning, experimenting with variations. Every day would be a new discovery, every day I would tweak the method a little. Hemant would come every now and then. When there were disasters, he would point out what could possibly have gone wrong.

Time began to fly. I was full of wonder. Soap-making sounded much easier than it was. For instance, the temperature had to be right. We learnt the hard way that fresh ingredients could not be put in just like that. They had to be treated or they would spoil. Milk had to be kept on ice. It also had to be parboiled. Each batch of soap needed to be left for four weeks to cure before being ready for use. We gave each batch that much time, though it tested my patience greatly!

The three-member troupe of candle-makers was now a three-member troupe of soap-makers.

They were the first team of what would later become Forest Essentials.

The soaps looked pure. They had the natural fragrance of real essential oils. After their resting period of four weeks, they had a creamy lather when they were used.

We wrapped them the old-fashioned way in brown paper, tied with raffia. And we stuck labels on them, on which I wrote the ingredients we had used to make them.

At first, we sent some of our soaps to close friends and family to try out. They seemed to like them a lot. And the demand continued.

And the soaps began to sell. Steadily.

Ritu oversaw the back end. Malathiji provided the reliability for our accounts. After all, what we spent, what we earned and what we saved would keep us steady on our course.

Hemant's interest and experience was our support in the experiments to make our products better and better. The successes and the errors were morphing into a system that ensured a quality standard. Ayurvedic doctors were now regularly overseeing the research and development.

Ayurveda has a different vision. The phrase 'research and development' does not fully conceptualize that vision. Ayurveda is a body of knowledge gathered through experience at two levels for the overall well-being of the human being. It sees the human being as the body, the mind and the spirit. It, therefore, presupposes physical, emotional, mental and spiritual well-being as its ethos. There is the aspect of theory to this science—the first level.

And very importantly, there is the aspect of experimentation—the second level. An attitude, somewhat, of 'What best can we do with our knowledge, given the material, the place, the time and the requirement? Does it all come together to bring well-being at all levels?' If so, then the experiment being tried should be adopted. In this sense, Ayurveda is alive to changing times and situations. It is interactive with its user. In this way, it is open to evolving options.

Just theory could be too rigid and end up limiting options. Just experimentation would be vague, leaving Vaids without guidelines and information to prevent mistakes.

Incorporating these valuable concepts, I, as the conceptualizer, was a perpetually driven Chief of Operations. There were many moments of joy when something came out the way it was envisaged, but more moments of heartbreak when there were disasters, which had to be thrown into the garbage.

I remember one such landmark day: after many attempts at making a transparent soap (which was not happening), we did something inadvertently … and that did it! We created a transparent soap. The Ayurvedic principle of experimentation, trying—here was a living demonstration.

———

One day, my friend Guddu had come over. I was where I usually was nowadays, in my garage office. Everyone had taken to coming straight to the garage.

'This is here to stay, I can see,' she said, looking around. I was concentrating on the boiling concoction in front of me.

'Um hmm,' I said. 'Can you think of a name which is unusual, yet conveys purity, fresh, sourced from nature?'

I smiled like a kid, looking up at her for a second. 'Not "herbal", not "nature" … too common.'

'Well, I have to tell you that I was in New York recently and I stayed at the Trump Towers. They had a small line of products with a beautiful name. It was called Forest Essentials.'

I seemed to know those words somehow. 'That's it! That's the name.' I loved it! 'Forest Essentials. That's what it's going to be!'

I had no idea that many years later we would have trademark issues and would buy out the name eventually.

We registered the company. You will also have to register a logo, I was told at the time.

'Logo? Let me see.' I was at zero. Then I drew a circle, put the words 'Forest Essentials' around it. Another moment. Then, with a flash of inspiration, I drew a tree inside. It looked a bit like a Christmas tree. It was supposed to be a mango tree!

'What do you think of it?'

My loyal gang approved in a chorus. And so it was. We had our logo.

19

The Ultimate Oils

By now, it was 2002.

It came to me over time that Ayurveda would have all kinds of formulations that could be used for beauty products, not just soap.

So, I introduced a new project—researching what could further promote beauty from those ancient Ayurvedic texts. We would have to keep to what was required in this day and age. Our Vaids were on the job again. And that was how our second product emerged. It was fresh, cold-pressed, pure body-massage oils, taken out of a kolhu by hand. The ultimate oil nutrient, rich and unprocessed—the way it was meant to be—and is exactly the same today.

The oils needed containers. We sourced simple glass bottles with aluminium caps.

In the first few months, a lot of my time would go in writing out labels for each soap, often late into the night, because we did not have the quantities for printing out labels and also because I was the only one who had good handwriting!

After some more time, with the massage oils added to the soaps, no matter how fast I wrote my labels, it was not fast enough for our increased range. The quantities were becoming more serious. That was the time we started looking at printed labels. Simple and accurate like before. But printed.

By then, we had sought and got permission from a popular bookshop in Khan Market to display and sell our soaps. We introduced a small batch of massage oils in that place for the first time, along with the soaps.

———

Sam came back from the US in 2002. He had started working in a multinational company in India.

After a few months, he came up to me one day and said, 'Mom, I want to join your company.'

'Don't do that, Sam, it's not large enough to take you in.' He was doing well. Why would he want to reinvent his career wheel with our little enterprise?

But he was keen. He kept coming back to it.

'What about a salary? I can't pay you.'

'Pay me when you can,' he said readily. I thought about it. That's not why I had sent him abroad to study. He was meant for better things. He wore me down with his insistence, making me go against my better judgement.

So, Forest Essentials got another employee, Sam. So far, we were Malathiji, Vikram, Diwan—our new recruit—and Ritu. Then Sanjay Singh joined us that year, in 2003. He took charge of accounts. His exacting standards in his work were soon quite visible. This freed Malathiji from accounts at least. She still handled most things for me, especially purchasing, which was key.

Looking back, Forest Essentials seems like a third child, after Sam and Diviya; and like a child born much later, it had all my attention. Also, like a sibling born much later, it had the attention and time of my children—of Sam who was settling down, and of Diviya, too, who had more time to participate again.

And like every child, this one too had a destiny of its own. Its destiny seemed to be unfolding.

20

'If You Cannot Eat It, Do Not Put It on Your Skin'

If you cannot eat it, do not put it on your skin. Here is the simple and profound principle of Ayurveda that, to me, makes all the difference every time. And so, Forest Essentials got one more guiding principle—often, you can eat the raw ingredients that we use in our products.

Another year had passed. Our Vaids were on their research. Another workable concept for today's times emerged. Ubtans. For soft clear skin.

What were these Ubtans? The purest, freshest traditional cleansers for the skin. They were to be made of sun-dried and then hand-pounded herbs. The process needed time and physical effort, like all our products so far.

I knew Ubtans was our next focus. The first Forest Essentials Ubtan came out as early as 2003. Slowly, we introduced variations of these, according to skin concerns, by changing the herbs and the mediums in each formulation.

I was asked in the beginning about why would we spend so much time and effort into the making of a cleanser which was basically just a utilitarian product? It was just used to wash the face, so why these elaborate processes and so much detail? Again, I feel that my thoughts then and now have not changed. The very fact that this was a product that you were to use at least once or twice a day, every day, meant that it had to be the most pure natural product possible.

Cleaned meticulously; with some ingredients sun-dried and some dried in the shade; using fresh herbs, flowers and roots; and finally pounded to a certain consistency, an Ubtan was the traditionally perfect cleanser for every woman, man or child. A little liquid was needed to blend it, generally either fresh milk or yoghurt. Readily available for most people in their kitchens, this made it possible to be personalized for each skin type. Certain mixers were traditionally recommended for various concerns, including tomato juice for pigmented skin, neem-infused water kept overnight for acne and so on. This was introduced by Forest Essentials in the market, again where it did not exist, except those that were made at home with tedious preparation. We still make it in small batches to preserve its freshness and incidentally, it is one of our most popular facial cleanser categories today, underlying the fact that ancient wisdom works.

What was emerging, along with each of our products, was an underlying principle of Ayurveda—respect for the senses—the Panchmahabhutas. Taste, touch, smell, sight and sound. Products should be in harmony with these senses. That was the year we brought out our Milk Baths. Milk has been used in Ayurveda to hydrate the skin and provide it with just enough fat to plump it up to youthfulness. We made Milk Baths in rose and jasmine fragrances, using extracts from fresh petals of both flowers.

These baths are still available today, personalized for clients on order.

Our Date and Litchi Youth Formula, a much later arrival, is a good example of the same Panchmahabhutas principle: it tastes of the juices of litchi and pulp of date, it has a honeyed milk colour, a delicious smell, a silken texture—and so, it addresses all the senses. It is hand-mixed to the chants of mantras, which infuse positivity into the cream. It has won many awards since, confirming the effectiveness of generations of use.

21

The Hyatt and Marco Polo

We were still early birds in 2004. And those were our very early days. Our products continued to sit on shelves in our little section inside a bookstore. This way, we now had an interface with the public, with the market, instead of just word of mouth.

From that vantage point, we kept getting inquiries and more orders. We later also started a small store at the Ambawatta One Complex in Mehrauli, Delhi, which had a new shopping buzz in those days.

It was good to see appreciation for the real thing. People were willing to pay for quality.

One day, I got a call from The Hyatt Regency in Delhi. They had a new General Manager from overseas who wanted to meet with us. I told Sam. We both went to the meeting later that week.

He said, 'Recently, someone gave me a gift. Of soaps. Forest Essentials.'

'Um hmm.' We nodded.

'I really enjoyed using the soap, so I made some inquiries.'

We nodded again. We waited with bated breaths and looked up at him.

'I want to introduce a product line in our hotels, which is not the usual substandard amenities that are supplied to hotel chains. I wanted to try your company's products for this.'

'Sure,' I said, completely clueless about how that could be done at all.

Sam shifted uneasily in his chair and tried not to glare at me.

'Good. Then we are on … Could you give us a trial round of the usual?'

I looked at him and raised my eyebrows.

'You know, the usual line—shampoo, conditioner, body lotion, shower gel and soap?'

We both stared at him. Before Sam could say anything about the fact that we did not do shampoos, conditioners, lotions and gels, I said, 'Yes, of course we can.'

'Okay. Wonderful. Give me some samples and I will see how I can work out an order for you.'

'Thank you. Mr Fulton, please give me two to three weeks to get back to you.'

'I'm actually travelling abroad,' he said, 'and will be back in a month. Let me have them then.'

We came out of the meeting and Sam said to me, 'What are you saying, Mom? How on earth are we going to give him samples? Do you have any idea? We don't make them.'

'Well, Sam. Here's where we start. We have to find out how to make really good-quality lotions and gels. We did make the soaps, didn't we?'

It was crazy. But he saw what I meant. He went along with it.

Then the whole process started again—the discoveries were amazing. It was the same thing as the soaps: it appeared that many large companies would add bleached waste machine oils, synthetic scents and colours. They would then add stone dust to increase weight. The soap cost ten rupees in the market. These would be made in bulk, packed, labelled and sold.

I found a small contract manufacturer for my Hyatt trial.

'Can you make these according to my specifications?'

He said no. 'We can take your order and supply to you but the specifications will be ours.'

'Please make them with our ingredients. We can do a trial order. You can keep your margins so that you are not at a loss,' I said.

In the end, he agreed. We got a small order made with our oils, some herbs, some infusions, all according to the specifications of our Ayurvedic doctors. It was only later that the manufacturer saw that we were actually going to sell what we had made. After that, he began to be much more forthcoming.

In the meantime, we did manage to give Hyatt their samples within a month. They were delighted. Of course, so were we. The volumes were larger than anything we had done before. New challenges were before us now.

The garage would not work any more. It was time for us to move out.

We found a small office in Shahpur Jat, behind our Panchsheel house. It was in a narrow lane with no space for a car to enter. We had three small rooms, which became our offices. Upstairs was a larger room, which became our warehouse.

We worked out of there for almost three years. Looking back, it never seemed like work. We were all always so excited about some new order or some new product and many days and nights were spent with our small team, who were all more enthusiastic than experienced.

Hyatt started us off with its Delhi hotel. We took another place in Shahpur Jat on rent where we could handle the growing volume and the variety that we were producing. We called it our factory.

Soon, we were supplying to the other Hyatt hotels—Kolkata, Mumbai ... And what began with soap turned into all amenities required for a hotel room.

Meanwhile, we had to be on top of our game as I saw it.

I scoured different markets and little-known shops in far-flung corners of our country—the diversity, first-hand, was unbelievable. Each culture brought some nuance to what we were trying to discover.

I immersed myself in the world of traditional skincare, looking at products, learning new methods and understanding techniques.

I watched for the little practical details that bring refinement and finesse, things that mould the product the way you want it to look, to feel. I watched displays, asked questions, took notes, observed, studied, many times till midnight.

I had heard, some time ago, from one of our senior Vaids about a small village in the South, around a hundred miles from Cochin, where a husband and wife used to prepare recipes handed down over generations.

He had also told me of some miraculously effective products that were painstakingly made by them according to Vedic principles. He knew the name of the village but not their names, and said that he had visited them four or five years earlier, but did not know if they still lived there. I was very intrigued as this was the kind of thing I was looking for. But a village in the back of beyond? No name or address? I decided that we must take a chance and at least try.

'Malathiji, we should go and see if we can find them,' I told her.

So the trip to Kerala was planned and both of us reached Cochin and then left for the village. It was a crazy situation, as we kept getting different directions and then realized that we were going around in circles! It was already six hours since we had left Cochin.

'Driver, do you know where we are?' I asked him.

'No, ma'am,' he replied honestly. 'I think we are lost.'

We were all hungry and thirsty. Then we saw a coconut seller going down the road.

'Stop stop,' I said. 'Let's get some coconut water.' We stopped the coconut seller. He cut off the tops of three coconuts and handed them to us. We drank the fresh, cool water with relief.

The driver was talking to him and suddenly we saw the coconut seller nodding his head vigorously. He was pointing to the left and explaining something. The driver came back. 'I have the directions. He knows the village,' he announced. Finally, we were on the way!

We reached the village at around four in the evening. Malathi spoke to some people and made inquiries. The husband and wife seemed to be quite well-known. One man offered to lead us to their home. When we reached, an elderly man was sitting outside on a charpoy. He had a serene face and greeted us with a charming smile and a namaste.

We tried to explain to him what we were looking for and, though the language was a barrier, we could understand each other in some fashion. He called out to his wife and she brought hot coffee in stainless steel tumblers. She also sat down with us. Haltingly, we asked about the special recipes we heard they made. The driver was also called to assist in the conversation.

The lady then called out to her son. He came out and I tried to explain to him that if they could produce those recipes for us, we could buy from them. He said, 'I understand. I will talk to Amma and Appa and I'm sure we can do it. I have been asking my parents to do something with their knowledge for many years.'

'I didn't realize that you speak English,' I said wonderingly.

'Yes, I have studied in the Christian school in Cochin,' he told me.

He explained that in their family they had undertaken this work to benefit society. Gradually, it turned out to be a treasure trove! Once I had explained what we wanted to do and needed authentic traditional formulations, they were incredibly receptive. These recipes had been handed down from father to son, from poultices for pain and arthritis, pastes using fresh herbs for skin ailments, stretch marks and pigmentation, roots infused in aged ghee for glowing skin and directions on how to infuse real silk into bath soaps.

They then brought out dried leaves on which the actual recipes were written. The leaves were fragile and wrapped in muslin, but the intricate handwriting was still quite clear.

I could not believe it! I tried to work out how we could use these and if they could make larger quantities for us. They were not sure because the ingredients were seasonal and they did not have much help. We spent another hour with them and exchanged numbers, telling them that we would be in touch with our exact requirements.

When we left them, I was trembling with excitement and exhaustion. We reached Cochin at around two in the morning.

This family went on to become one of our key suppliers and built their business with us. The father has since passed away, but his ideals remain, with their meticulous attention to detail and adherence to ancient ritualistic methods of preparation. It is these which give the products their extraordinary effectiveness.

We then work on the textures, fragrances and delivery of the products to make them easier to apply, and more pleasurable—and it remains as it was envisioned so many generations ago.

Back in Delhi, demand was increasing for our products. Gradually, other clients also got added to the ever-growing list that year. I felt as though we had, in Forest Essentials, a rather clever little baby to bring up. It was doing rather well for its age in playschool.

We now serviced several hotel chains. We only took orders from five-star category hotels, which is a standard I had set in the very beginning, and which was questioned on many occasions later as it did impact our growth, but I never deviated from this. Things now seemed to follow a trajectory: the hotels started cautiously with our retail products—our soaps, our spa products like the massage oils, diffuser oils, gift sets.

Then, without fail, they would want all the amenities for their rooms from us.

Around that time, we also took in a partner. He actually just appeared in our life.

Mahesh Patel was an NRI Gujarati who had come to do business in India in pharmaceuticals. He had just sold his company and was looking to invest in other ventures.

Even though it was only the start for us at Forest Essentials, he thought our business had potential. We gave him twenty per cent of our shareholding. We had taken to him and his wife Usha immediately. Mahesh had a keen business sense. This would work.

And it has done to this very day. We are more family today with Mahesh and Usha than just business partners.

Around the same period, our growing business demanded more structure, more professionalism.

That year, we began to hold our first board meetings. My cousin's husband, more in the role of an elder brother, Abhay Yograj—Yog to me—offered to chair these for us. In spite of his extremely busy work life, he helped us shape the nature of our new initiatives, making it possible for us to move forward in a clear and orderly direction.

He showed us how important it was to have processes. Yog's steering of our ship has been invaluable, both to the company and to us individually. He is not there today but much of his advice still guides us and we miss him dearly.

With Yog, we developed another relationship. His daughter, Shona, was studying in New York when Sam went to America, and he had asked her to look out for him. Shona became the elder sister Sam never had and rescued him from many a dire situation. They have a bond that has survived the trials and tribulations both have gone through in their earlier lives.

22

Tirupati

I cannot write this book without a mention of Balaji, the Supreme God of Tirupati, and my incredibly intense encounter with Him. For someone who had only visited Gurudwaras while growing up, going to Tirupati was a revelation.

I had gone once, when we lived in Madras and I was a few months pregnant with Sam, but it was not a happy experience. I remember being sick all the way there and all the way back, with no recollection of the Darshan.

Now, it was 2005. I had just come back from a trip somewhere and got a call from Guddu. She said, 'We are leaving for Tirupati tomorrow morning and there is one seat free in the helicopter. Shiv, Mummy and I are going. Do you want to come?'

My first reaction was to refuse. I had never really wanted to go, and this was too rushed. But strangely, as I was about to say no, I found myself saying, 'Oh okay, I'll come.' *How odd was that*, I thought, but it was done.

We went to Tirupati and of course, the Darshan had been arranged by Shiv, who is an ardent devotee. The first time I didn't realize what a big deal it was to have time with just us there, while the priests performed the puja and we were in the presence of Lord Balaji Himself. It was an overwhelming experience—there was some connection, which was beyond my comprehension. For the first time since my father's death, I had the feeling of being with someone who was saying, 'Relax. Leave it to me. I will take care of everything.'

I came out and started crying. It was a huge release. I had tears streaming down and was sobbing uncontrollably.

'Are you okay? What has happened?'

We sat down and I said I was fine—it just was the strangest kind of relief. I came back from there with something having changed indelibly in my life.

After that I made a few trips—never initiated by me but by circumstances—which came together so fortuitously that it seemed it was time for me to go again. The trips were always phenomenal, and we had incredible Darshans, where we had the fortune to be in close proximity to Him without the huge chanting crowds. I always came back blessed and re-energized.

Then another trip happened a few years ago. We were going with some friends who had arranged a Darshan. Savita, a friend of mine, and I were coming in from Delhi. Unfortunately, the flight got delayed and we missed the Darshan. The others were catching a flight back but I didn't want to leave without seeing Lord Balaji.

'You will have to wait till the next morning for me to arrange a Darshan again, Mira,' said my friend Sanjiv. 'Now it is only the regular Darshan for all the people waiting.'

'No problem, Savita and I will do the regular Darshan. Can't do special ones all the time,' I said, completely oblivious to what it entailed. He did try to dissuade me, but I was adamant and said we would go and take the evening flight back.

We went to the booth where the tickets were sold and bought two tickets for Rs 500 each. Then we stood in the line, which seemed to be stretching interminably each time I glanced back.

Savita smiled. 'Miru, such fun!'

'Yes, Savvy, so good to do things on our own.'

We started walking down the corridor towards the temple.

The first time that we realized something was wrong was when we went through the first arch and someone pushed us both. I turned—it was a huge man in a lungi, sweating profusely and shouting, 'Govinda!'

Soon, the chant was reverberating through the whole courtyard and there were thousands and thousands of people who were packed together like sardines. After almost twenty minutes, we thought, *Let's get out of here.* We tried everything but we couldn't move. Not in front and not at the back. We were pushed forward in jerks, unable to breathe properly in the mass of humanity which was in a fever of devotion.

Rickshawallahs, coolies, families, children, groups of young men, the elderly and infirm—there was everyone—it was beyond a nightmare! It went on and on, we didn't know where we were and how long it would take. Finally, after what seemed like four or five hours, we were pushed in front of Balaji for a second, with the line in hysterics and the priests not allowing anyone to even attempt to take a glance. It was enough that you had passed through those portals! We were outside minutes later in the cool air.

It was not till much later that I understood. He wanted me to know that it was not that simple to get His Darshan. I had not realized the enormity of what it actually meant until we were caught that day in the thronging crowds that waited patiently for days to just get a glimpse of Him.

I have gone many times since—in comfort, to Darshans beautifully arranged by close friends, including my dear friend Pinky Reddy, who has some other almost spiritual connection with me—but I have never forgotten that it only happens when He wishes it to, and I appreciate every moment of it.

23

Khan Market

It was at this time that Sadeev Sandhu, a very old and dear family friend, came up with a proposition. He owned a lot of property in Khan Market; in fact, the bookstore where we had a counter was a tenant of his. He called me and said, 'Mira, there is a store coming up on rent in Khan Market, which is rare. If you are interested, I can put you in touch with the owner.'

A full store, in prime Khan Market! It was a wild and exciting possibility.

I asked Sadeev to come over. I called Sanjay, my loyal Accountant, to understand the financials. After understanding we had to make a substantial deposit, I asked Sanjay, 'Do you think we can afford it? Can we justify it?'

His answer was, 'Ma'am, we must try or we will never know.'

I still trust Sanjay's judgement implicitly, as I did that day.

I thought briefly of the possibility of it not succeeding—but it was a flash. I had already made up my mind.

Sadeev, Sanjay, Sam and I decided to take the plunge.

Sadeev negotiated with the landlord and we said we had to take a leap of faith. The numbers were alarming, it was our first real store.

The same uncertainty that we had come up against at each new stage appeared. We constantly fell down, unable to see something until it was in our face—we were supposed to know what sales we were expecting, we were supposed to know how to stock, how to train staff, how to keep store staff, how to handle back-end supplies ... we had no clue!

I called Vikram: 'Vicky, we have taken a store in Khan Market, please help. I need a simple elegant design—not ornate.' He came over.

We set up the store ourselves from start to finish. We could barely afford the rent so time was of the essence, but our enthusiasm was overflowing. Such technicalities! Prakash came in as our new Warehouse Supervisor. He was brought in by Mahesh. It was the only way we could determine how much stock could fill the shelves.

Then we needed a Manager for the store. I thought of the perfect one for the job—my friend Savita, who was from an old Delhi family. She was widowed and living alone. Her children were abroad. I asked her if she would manage the store for us. She was very happy to.

It was an unusual store. The staff was different—we sought out good people from good backgrounds, who loved what they did. It was a calculated risk to start with such expenses.

On the first day, however, our entire stock at Khan Market was sold out.

There was a mad scramble to restock the next day. It was the same the next day and the next. And it continued. In those days, I felt like a newbie learning to rollerblade—frightened and excited at the same time. We had no idea about inventory, no idea about retailing, no idea about anything. Each one of us had to learn on the job. And we were in it together.

When I look at it in retrospect—the Khan Market store seems a bit unreal. If we had thought about it, it would not have happened. The reality was that we had no retail experience—forget retail, we had no experience on how to sell, how to display or process for billings! The only person who had worked in a chemist store earlier was our Supply Chain Warehouse recruit, so we all turned to him for advice. Firstly, he only knew stocking the way it was done in pharmacies— so there were rows and rows of products. When I saw the dozens and dozens of products stocked one next to the other and behind, I said, 'This does not seem right'. 'No, ma'am,' said our new recruit. '*Aise hi hota hai retail mein.*' It still didn't seem right. So I climbed on the ladder to the top shelf and started removing products. Yes, that was better. '*Nahi nahi, ma'am. Ab toh shelf bikul khali lag raha hai. Sab sochenge ki humare pass kuch stock nahi hai!*' I convinced Prakash that the three or four products on each shelf looked much more premium and they only had to keep replacing it (if it sold!) from the back room. So everyone in the store who believed that I was wrong reluctantly removed stock from the shelves. When people started coming in and loved the minimalistic look, it became everyone's else's collective idea, which was fine.

The how-to-sell was only common sense and I became the de facto trainer who had no idea how to sell. However, I applied some basic rules which were: Never come on too strong. Explain the product and listen to what the client wants. Listen was the operative word. Most people don't listen to what exactly the other person wants, or doesn't. Never recommend anything to anyone which you don't feel works for them, just to sell it. It will not work in the long run and they will not come back. When you present someone a product, it should be done with care, thoughtfully wrapped and beautifully presented. We were the first to add fresh flowers and neem leaves into our carry bags. Even the neem leaves were cleaned and dried just so, so they still looked fresh but were not brittle. Finally, we sprayed some scented mist over the bag, which added the delight factor.

But there was one thing that I knew clearly—how our clients must be treated. For my clients, buying in our store had to be a luxurious experience in itself.

Each visitor got time, attention and an atmosphere inside the store. If he or she bought a product, they got it wrapped in sweet scented crisp tissue, sprinkled over with fresh flower petals and neem leaves, inside an attractive paper bag. I would personally train each boy and each girl that showed up for the sales work in the store—how they were to talk, how they were to wrap the products, how a ribbon was to be tied to the handle of the bag ... I would be there every day to witness the processes for myself. The size of the neem leaf, the colours of the flowers—all had to be perfect.

As the days passed, Savita began to call me whenever there was a well-known face visiting our shop. Gradually, it started becoming a daily occurrence:

'Today Priyanka Gandhi came to make a basket for her mother's birthday.'

'So-and-so wanted a wedding gift.'

'Mrs X wanted to gift this to someone who is travelling abroad.'

Every day we used to get frantic calls: 'We have no stock—send quickly.' It was time to learn inventory management—how to restock, how to forecast sales ...

Within three months, we realized that the Khan Market store was a success. A success that had no strategy and no future business plan as yet. We began to get different kinds of opportunities for greater exposure to our brand—a counter in larger stores, in pharmacies, in good grocery shops.

This would immediately make us visible and accessible everywhere, in ready, standing stores. I was overwhelmed by those offers. They promised quick results.

But that voice in my head was speaking as usual. And it had the same clarity that had led me till here: Forest Essentials was more than a product. It was an experience. A luxurious feeling of well-being. Our products were one part of the whole thing. We needed our own store to create that experience.

We needed our ethos to speak when a potential client came to us— right from how he or she felt when they entered, to how they felt with our salespeople, to when they browsed through the shelves, to when they tried a product, to when they used each one of the products. At each step, they had to feel special … Our first store had shown me the importance of our own space whose quality we controlled.

So, the route I decided was for Forest Essentials to have its own stores.

I fully realized that this would take longer, that this was likely to be harder. Yet, I knew that it would be worthwhile, that there was no other way to be Forest Essentials.

Sam agreed with me. To say no to the many offers was difficult but we did it.

The front end—the selling—began to settle down and become a predictable manageable process over time.

We made mistakes, we incurred costs because of them, but we were also learning the right ways. After that the next phase was to concentrate on the back end. The back end was production.

24

Lodsi

That same year, we came out with Body Polishes—they were hand-churned with raw cane sugar crystals, butters and oils mixed with essential oils. The ethos of well-being, even decadence, begins to speak when you see delicious sugar crystals gently exfoliating your skin while the lingering fragrance of essential oils pleasures your senses …

Shahpur Jat was overrun by the burgeoning load of orders. It would not be enough any more.

To me, this was not a problem, just an indication that the time had come for my second vision to be made a reality. When I started out with my vision of creating pure, high-quality nourishing products for the body, no matter what the price, I had in mind another equally intuitive vision—that somehow this work should benefit people at the grass roots.

That it should most benefit the more suppressed of those people—women. In this case, the local women in the villages from where we sourced raw materials.

We were already linked to our caretaker at Rishikesh, Bacchan Singh's village, Lodsi, up the mountain above our property. Those villagers had built our Rishikesh home years ago. Much of our raw material, many of our Vaids, our know-how, were already coming from these ancient unspoilt environs. Lodsi was there, nestled at a height amongst waterfalls and springs. It was part of one of the several forested mountains around our home there. The women of the village would find it easy to work at our workshop in the village.

The equipment was traditional. The method was traditional—growing and collecting organic raw material, fresh herbs and flowers, cold-pressing oil from raw material using a kolhu, following the recipes. They would be trained by us, in order to keep exacting standards.

They would be safe in their village and would be able to earn their own money.

But, as usual, it was not easy. We were stumped by an unexpected challenge.

The women were not allowed to work outside of their homes in the village. This was understandable because every society finds its own system of harmony within its circumstances. How, I wondered, were we to offer a greater harmony where the village would see that this change would benefit them greatly while benefitting our business as well?

We started preparing for working out of huts in Lodsi. At first, we got no response from any of the women. Some of the men used to work at our home in Rishikesh.

I decided that we should approach the problem through the men. If we made the men understand the benefit of the arrangement, then the women would slowly feel more free to come forward. I met with some of the men we knew and went with them to meet the village Patwari. I explained exactly what we wanted to do and how we would pay men and women equal wages, a revolutionary idea in those days. We convinced them that the women would be completely safe and would work with the villagers, most of whom were their husbands, brothers or related to them in some way.

Then, we were allowed to speak to the women. We told them that they would be earning their own money. They could not understand this. We left them with the idea and waited.

First, two women came. They learned the work, which was simple, considering the hard tasks they were used to. Then, at the end of that fateful first month, we opened bank accounts for both of them. In their presence, we deposited their month's salary into the accounts for them.

'No one else can touch it?' they asked wonderingly.

'No one.'

From having husbands who could take whatever they wanted in return for letting them live, to being able to save money for themselves and their children, was incomprehensible in the beginning.

As time went by, they began to talk about it: it was, they said later, the most liberating experience in the world.

We soon had two more, then five more, then ten more and so our workforce grew. Today, all those years later, we always have a waiting list of women who want to join our perpetually full team.

———

But in 2005, things were different from what they are now. Building in Lodsi seemed to be an insurmountable challenge.

'Ma'am, we understand your concern for Lodsi but ... it's an almost ninety-degree climb straight up the mountain dirt track to reach.'

'How are we to reach the raw materials there?'

'How are we to bring the ready products down?'

'We'll bring them down the way the villagers would do it,' I said. 'We'll ask them what we need to do ... mules ... men ... whatever ... what's so difficult!'

'How are we to build permanent structures there? Which contractor can do that, ma'am? No one will be willing!'

'Okay. We will find a way,' I said.

When it rained, or during the winter months, it seemed as if this was the most tedious, harrowing, exhausting enterprise.

Why a remote mountain village perched high up inside a tangled Himalayan forest for production? I sometimes questioned my own judgement. But somewhere it was God's plan—because none of them left me.

In fact, they trudged and struggled through rain and frost without questioning. They are family. Even family loses its faith sometimes. But they never did. We were blessed. I have always been grateful for the generosity of their faith in us and belief in their work. I believe they sensed this and still do, to this day.

25

Towards a Juggernaut

Bhringraj, brahmi, japapatti and amla are fruit, flowers and roots associated in India with healthy, long, lustrous hair. Our Vaids confirmed their medicinal, rejuvenating qualities. My mind would inevitably circle around what could add value to our luxurious version of Ayurveda.

The answer was upon us that year, 2006—haircare. We began cautiously working to perfect a single product for hair. We brought out our traditional Bhringraj Head Massage Oil. Most Indian homes know this oil. I remember seeing it ever since I can remember, a thick, viscous oil regarded as a necessary evil for beautiful hair.

From our grandmothers to our household help, women have been protecting and maintaining their hair using this concoction. Over the years, commercial practices have led it to be made using synthetic scents covering up inexpensive, substandard ingredients. But it was packaged and affordable.

We came out with the original version, using bhringraj, amla and brahmi herbs mixed with the correct oils in the recommended traditional proportions. Every herb was picked fresh, cleaned and sun-dried. It was then infused into large vats of cold-pressed oils of coconut and sesame, coconut milk and other specified ingredients. These were simmered for days over slow fires so that all their properties were absorbed. Forest Essentials' Bhringraj Head Massage Oil was pure, enjoyable to use and hugely beneficial. Just like the original recipe.

———

The Shahpur Jat office and warehouse section were becoming inadequate now. Our playschool baby was beginning to look like a juggernaut. Around the end of that year, we moved to a larger office in Noida.

To deal with the juggernaut, we separated into sections—hotels, retail, marketing, purchase, supply chain. Each department now had an in-charge and their own team.

Having no preconceived notions on how to do business was in some ways a good thing. Since there is no road map, you can improvise and experiment with no sense of impending disaster. One learning was that I went deep into anything that I wanted to do. I asked, I learnt, I read as much as I could. Nothing was too minor and I did it myself before delegating it to anyone else. Also, anyone to whom it was delegated knew I could check on them. When businesses become large, inevitably everyone takes on some part and there can be instances of 'I did it but the other person did not give me what was required to complete it.' The process then takes much longer, through many levels, and there are very few people who take responsibility by saying, 'The buck stops here.' The agility you have when you are growing a business is a huge advantage, helping to minimize mistakes and capitalize on the right decisions.

Looking back on the key difficulties when we were building the business, one was packaging. Packaging in India was always based on large quantities, which was a huge problem for us, as our quantities were very low. This included bottles, caps, labels and pretty much everything in between. We had to improvise by getting small lots of available generic bottles and using basic craft paper for packaging and labels.

A great deal of time had to be spent with various suppliers, scheduling them for small quantities while promising them larger orders in the future and assuring them—and ourselves—that this would happen as soon as the company grew.

It eventually turned out to be a combination of grit, perseverance and charm. Sourcing raw material was again a huge issue because of lower quantities and our insistence on high-quality ingredients. Most suppliers kept sacks of herbs stored for months in unhygienic conditions. The herbs that were prescribed in Vedic texts, which we required for our formulations, had to be freshly picked, stored in certain conditions and used within a certain period of time. If this was not done, the effectiveness and potency of the herb could not be utilized. We needed to know how we could source fresh herbs. This was a huge challenge. It took us a long time to actually find sources from where we could get the herbs directly, immediately after they had been plucked, as opposed to buying them from suppliers. The process sounds easier than it was, and it was one of our most difficult requirements to fulfil when we started out. Looking back, this is what took time, energy and unflagging determination—to be able to think that we could and must resolve this issue, without which nothing else would work.

In the end, it was relationships that evolved with people on the ground that made it possible for this to happen. Going to places where these activities actually took place, in areas which we did not know of, and meeting with people who we couldn't believe existed. This did not take money, just time and single-minded focus.

26

Branding

I think one of the fundamental reasons why Forest Essentials became a successful brand was because I was always extremely critical about how it was perceived. Branding was something I always supervised myself and we had very strict guidelines. There were many opportunities we lost because the brand was being depicted in too much of a mass-market manner for my liking; it did not always seem so to everyone else, but this was something I would personally not negotiate on. It limited us in many ways, and we took longer to reach where we wanted, but I would do the same if I had a choice again. We took no shortcuts. It had to be the best or nothing. This permeated down from our sourcing to our making techniques to our associations and finally to the actual presentation and sale of the product.

I am not sure when Neha Gadi joined us, but she went through the ranks diligently to become Head—Institutional Sales much later. I bring up Neha's name here because she is an integral part of the company. Brand perception was one of the issues we were not completely aligned on. Understandably, since her job was to get more business, she could not comprehend my approach. 'Ma'am, how can we refuse this business? It will add to our top line. You cannot imagine how important it is for us,' she would say.

'Neha, it does not fit into our guidelines. Let it go. The hotels you want also want exclusivity and for them branding is key as well. Don't dilute it,' I would tell her.

It took many years and many disagreements but recently Neha said to me, 'I now understand. If you hadn't been so clear, we would not be where we are today!'

Incredibly goal-focused and passionate about her work, she has been so much a part of Forest Essentials, through getting married, having a much-awaited son and navigating a challenging yet satisfying career.

———

If I was the one with the vision for Forest Essentials, the team evolved its own strategy. Noida was where we all converged.

It was 2006. Diviya had been working with us off and on about a year after she got married. She joined us full time that year. She found her niche in the graphics and design side of our product packaging.

When I look back at Diviya's induction into the company, it has been quite a hair-raising ride. It was just she and one more person in graphics, both of whom were reasonably inexperienced but hugely enthusiastic. They gradually progressed to executing all the window displays for the stores and in-house photoshoots.

Being a brand that stressed on seasonal became a nightmare to actually execute. The budgets started out as non-existent and gradually came to some sort of median level. The first few stores required much more effort and detailing since there were no standard operating procedures, and each shape and size was different, which had to be done individually. In retrospect, I wonder how she managed, since the timelines always seemed to be yesterday. Understanding and creating visuals which were in line with the very strict brand guidelines was not easy, given the fact that there were no set formats like established brands. Diviya being Diviya, she took it in her stride.

27

Warden Road

My friend Vasundhara Raje had a girlfriend in Mumbai who had a retail store she wanted to rent out.

We were discussing something else when the words 'space' and 'rent' caught my attention. Weren't we ready to sell in Mumbai? We were.

'Rent? A space in Mumbai?' I asked.

'You want to open in Mumbai?'

'I would like to meet her, Vasu. We are looking to retail in Mumbai.'

'Sure,' she said.

I got in touch with the Mumbai friend. After much back and forth, we decided on the days that suited us both. I set everything aside and fixed a date for going to finalize the renting of her property for a Forest Essentials store.

We would now appear in a new city. I was excited. The appointment was set. Everything was organized.

We reached Mumbai. The store was in Cuffe Parade. *Nice,* I thought.
I called her, excited to get a Mumbai store for Forest Essentials.

Strangely, she was not picking up my call. A few hours and several
calls later, she came on the line. There was a problem. From her
hesitation and her excuses, I knew that she had changed her mind. 'I
am really sorry, Mira, but I had promised someone earlier and …'

'That's fine,' I said, putting the phone down. I was determined not
to go back without a store in Mumbai. I told our first employee in
Mumbai, a young man called Sachin whom we had hired a month
earlier, 'We have to rent some other place. This Cuffe Parade store is
not available.'

'Ma'am, I will ask around and get back to you as soon as I hear of
something.'

'Yes. Today or tomorrow latest.'

'What!' Sachin said. 'Ma'am, that's not poss—'

'Sachin, I am not going back now. You know you can do it. I know
only you can make it happen here!'

It turned out that Sachin knew one Hemant Bhai in the Royal
Medico Chemist at the Oberoi Hotel where we supplied spa products
and retail products in those days. Hemant Bhai was a Gujarati. Sachin
was talking to everyone he possibly knew about a space for our store.

'I know someone …' Hemant Bhai said. And that was, it turned
out, a very reluctant landlord who had been very dissatisfied with all
his tenants up till then. I went to meet him with Sachin.

'He is a Gujarati. An old man. Very reluctant to rent out,' Sachin
had told me.

'Where is the place?'

'On Warden Road. He will be hard to convince, ma'am.'

'Don't worry, Sachin. We'll do it,' I said. I extended my trip by two
days.

Hard or not, I was going to get this to work. I knew it was the place
for us. It had a prestigious address—Bhulabhai Desai Road in the
heart of South Mumbai. That space was a Forest Essentials one for me.

The 'cranky old Gujarati' and I formed an instant rapport. He had checked our financials before he had even met us. 'But you are very new,' he said. 'What if it doesn't work in Mumbai? How will you pay my rent?' I assured him that it would definitely work and we would take it for a year, for which we would pay the rent anyway. 'Okay, make sure my rent is paid on the first of every month. My wife liked the products Sachin gave us and she says it will do well, so I will take a chance.' Now, Forest Essentials was available in Mumbai.

We still have that first store, and it did do better than we expected!

The products were increasing. With each product our staff underwent complete training—a full understanding of the ingredients, the recipe and the method with which it was made, what the benefits were as promised by Ayurveda, how to make the best use of it.

I must add a fairly unusual incident here, in keeping with the unusual ethos of the book. Many years after we launched the store, there was a call at home on the landline which Karishma, my daughter-in-law, picked up. It was Sadashiv, our first store assistant from Mumbai at the Warden Road store. '*Ma'am se baat karni hai,*' he said.

'*Ma'am abhi busy hain, Sadu.*'

'*Karishma Ma'am, bahut zaroori hai,*' he said in hushed tones. '*Rekhaji baat karengi, store mein ayee hui hain.*'

'*Kaun Rekhaji?*' asked Karishma and then light dawned when she realized his awestruck tone. She came inside the study where I was sitting with some people and whispered, 'Mom, maybe you should take this one.'

'What is so important, K?' I asked but I took the call. Rekha's inimitably husky voice that said how much she loved the products was exactly the voice I had heard over the years in endless blockbusters. It was the start of an unlikely friendship. We spoke sporadically, sometimes briefly, sometimes we had long chats over the years. On life, the children, a new launch, the best recipe to make brass shine (a common passion!). We would always say we must meet, but it somehow never happened with our schedules.

In November 2021, I said to her over a conversation, 'I'm going to Rishikesh, you must come.'

'Okay, actually, I will. Can't believe we haven't met!'

So she came—and was as elegantly beautiful as I had imagined her, even in her track pants and top knot of hair. Warm and spontaneous, she did yoga with Angad, my seven-year-old grandson, had long chats with all the children and chilled on the deck. It seemed as if we had always known her.

28

The Panchmahabhutas

In 2007, we brought out one of my favourite products—the Date and Litchi Youth Formula that I have described earlier. It responds to all the senses—taste, touch, sound, sight and smell, which is the basis of the Panchmahabhutas theory in the Vedas. This has been a secret formula that Indian women who could afford the painstaking preparation have used over the centuries.

It had a special process. Its ingredients had to be fresh or sun-dried and each one was blended in exact proportions according to the recipe. This mix was then buried in terracotta pots to ferment under the ground to enrich it with natural enzymes. The original recipe, which was not very legible, said, 'Bury under the ground, preferably under a banyan tree.' *Did they actually mean it, or were we misinterpreting it,* I wondered. I came to know much later that the banyan tree was recommended because of its shade as in ancient times, the scorching sun would have made it ferment faster than it should.

We still follow the same methods of preparation. This mixture is taken out when it is ready, hand-mixed in heavy metal pots and simmered over a slow fire. Chants are sung by the workers while the mixing is done to allow positive vibrations to be absorbed into the final product. What took several months to get ready is now available off the shelf! The same satisfaction, the same satin finish on the skin— effortlessly, deliciously silken.

———

The year 2007 was the beginning of another momentous association in the Forest Essentials story. That was the year that we began a relationship with Taj Hotels. It was a momentous turning point for us to get our amenities and other associated products into the Taj luxury hotels across India. It was not only the products but also getting supply-chain systems to efficiently dispatch them on time and build enough stocks. They wanted a unique fragrance that was both Indian and yet not too ethnic, to appeal to the global traveller. It was a challenge but in the end, we got it just right! We loved it and they were delighted.

Now, Taj hotel guests associate the fragrance of our Neem and Aloe Vera toiletries with the prestigious Taj hallmark experience.

However, it was getting clear that Lodsi would no longer be able to contain the demand. That was when we shortlisted some land to build a factory. We knew what we wanted but had no idea what setting up a factory with no experience entailed.

We went wrong with most things. We did not envisage proper storage. We listened to too many 'consultants', since we did not know better, ordered some redundant machinery. Everything that could possibly go wrong, did.

But the structure was up, and we slowly got it right. The amazing thing was that ninety-five per cent of our people had never worked in a factory before!

We had a fairly motley group of our first factory workers-to-be. Most were fresh out of the village—and others had done some carpentry and some electrical work. There was one who had worked in an oil-extraction unit, and he was our most qualified. The good thing is that they were all young, enthusiastic and willing to learn. A lot of tasks, strangely enough, they knew instinctively, including knowing what seeds, plants and herbs were harvested in what season, and how to sort and process by hand.

Diwan was the leader of the team by default, as he was always responsible for motivating the slower ones. Our first Body Polisher recipe, from a royal household where it was made for the women at home, was explained by me to him painstakingly, step by step. It was just not coming out right, until he said that step three should be after step four. 'Yeh toh tab hi mast banega.' And, of course, he was right. I am still not quite sure if he even knew what the Body Polisher was then but he was able to reproduce the exact texture and richness of the original product. The Sea Salt Rose Crystal Body Polisher has been consistently in the bestseller list from the beginning.

Each person we found had the most varied skills. Vikram was like clockwork. You knew his schedule and discipline to the minute, and could set your clock with him. Yuvraj had an innate sense of production; he knew exactly how much to heat something or allow it to cool completely. Awdhesh and Deepak fit effortlessly into Vikram's team. Surjan had an instinctive knack of presentation and could pack beautifully, like a trained professional.

A series of names runs past in my memory. Sometimes the faces are as clear as they were so many years ago, sometimes the names bring back an image that is sharply etched. Sanjit, Chait, Nitesh, Mohit, Sunil, Avtar, Manoj and so many more. The rough terrain, frequent landslides. The difficult learning from scratch—nothing fazed them. *'Chalo chalo, bhai. Agey nikalna hai.'* Always with a smile.

Mohan Lal, who was our young gardener with green fingers, found his forte in doing what he loved most—working with the freshest produce. He now heads production in our Lodsi factory, twenty years later.

Almost all the early factory workers are still with us today. Some are supervisors, some department heads and all in senior positions. Everyone owns their own house and is settled comfortably. I think the defining factor here is that there was recognition of skills, dignity of labour and respect for each and every one. In most large organizations, the worker and his immense contribution is faceless and unrecognized. In the days when R&D was notional, it was just me who did the research to check if a product was special enough for Forest Essentials to make. Many years ago when Anuj came on board, it was him and me, and he had the amazing ability to understand exactly what I wanted. Then Rajesh, who also had a fine sensibility, and then, of course, the many wonderful people who now make ours an unrivalled R&D team. In the last several years, all of them got periodical offers for double their salaries from companies that wished to reproduce the Forest Essentials products and feel—how difficult can it be, they must have thought? What they don't understand is that it is not just a product, but the philosophy of caring enough to give back on every level which makes it what it is. And happily, most of our staff does not care to leave.

Till 2007, at the end of every year, I would sit down and write out by hand individual notes wishing each employee in the company a happy new year, and talking about what we had achieved and wished to achieve in the next year. I am told that all who were there then still treasure every note. On every Diwali, I would find out each person's preferences, what they needed or what they liked, and buy gifts for them myself—'really needs a pressure cooker' or 'wants a new watch'. I never thought I was doing something out of the ordinary, because this is what I would do for my own family. Recollecting this later, and every time it is recounted, it sounds like a big deal, but it actually was not. It came from the heart and I enjoyed this exercise every year. I'm not sure exactly which year this stopped but it must have been around this time, because numbers were becoming larger and it was more than I could realistically have done myself. Finally, we needed an HR department!

29

The Estée Lauder Surprise

'Mom, where are you?' It was a call from Sam, from Mumbai. I had just got back to Delhi.

'I'm here. Anything the matter?'

'Well, I just got a call from Rohan Vaziralli, the Country Manager of Estée Lauder.'

'And?'

'And Mr Leonard Lauder, the Chairman of the company, is coming to Delhi and wants to meet with us.'

There was a moment of dead silence.

'You're joking. How come?'

'I don't know,' said Sam.

We fixed to meet at The Imperial, where Mr Lauder was staying in the presidential suite. We were met by Rohan who escorted us up to a small meeting room adjoining his suite. Rohan was young, impeccably dressed and obviously from a good family. There was a conference table in the centre of the room with six chairs around it. Rohan excused himself, saying he would just inform Mr Lauder that we were there. Sam and I looked at each other, not quite sure what to do or say.

Suddenly, the door opened, and it was Leonard Lauder. His personality dominated the whole room.

'I'm sure you're wondering why I have asked to meet with you?' he said in his disarming manner. 'I had been gifted some products of yours by Lady Lynn Rothschild. I loved them. I was keen to see who was behind the very interesting brand.'

He wanted to know how we'd started, what we were doing, how we made the products. In no time, we were chatting as if we had known each other for years.

He told us how his mother had started their company and how he, as a young man, started out by helping her. He used to write out the labels and put the cream into jars.

It was a fascinating story of her determination and his unerring intuition that took it ahead.

Suddenly, Rohan looked at his watch. 'Mr Lauder, you have a lunch appointment in about ten minutes.'

'Thank you, Rohan, I hadn't realized the time.'

It had been almost two hours! We were getting up to leave when he said, 'Mira, how do you see your company in ten years? What do you want it to be?'

'I want to do what you have done, Mr Lauder. I want it to be recognized as the best Ayurvedic beauty brand in the world.'

'Hmm,' he said. 'You know, you might actually do it. It was a pleasure meeting you and Sam and we will be in touch and see if we can do something which may be of mutual interest.'

We thanked him, said our goodbyes and left.

In the elevator, I said to Sam, 'Do you think this was real? Do you think that was actually Leonard Lauder?'

I was still unable to believe it.

'Yes, Mom, it was. No one is impersonating him!'

We came to know later that he had come to India to attend Elizabeth Hurley's wedding. Elizabeth Hurley had been for many years the face of Estée Lauder. Leonard Lauder made a stopover in Delhi on his private jet and, because of the Rothschild gift, actually went to visit our Khan Market store before meeting us! After the meeting, a few weeks later, I got a handwritten letter from him.

It was a beautifully written letter. And it said that he would send his business development team to India soon. He hoped we would meet up with them.

I have a thing for handwritten letters. I think it stemmed from the time my friend Nina's mother, Adarsh Aunty, used to send her the most beautiful letters when we were in boarding school. They were on exquisite notepaper with tissue-lined envelopes and it was the start of a lifelong obsession.

For some months, life continued as usual. We did not hear from them.

Then Sam was on his way to Barbados with some friends for a cricket match and they stopped over in New York. One of his college friends had made a reservation in a restaurant where apparently you had to book months in advance. When they reached for dinner, there was a small group of people ahead of them.

Suddenly, Sam recognized Mr Lauder with an elegantly dressed lady and another couple. Sam went up to him.

'Sam. How good to see you. What are you doing in New York?' Mr Lauder asked.

'I'm on my way to Barbados, sir,' said Sam.

He introduced Sam to his wife saying, 'Evelyn, do you remember that I spoke to you about Forest Essentials in India? This is Sam.'

She was very warm and then Mr Lauder enquired, 'Has my team been in touch yet?'

'Not yet, Mr Lauder.'

'Well, they will, soon.'

How random was that! To meet in the same restaurant out of the thousands of restaurants in New York on the same day and at the same time. It had to have been predestined.

Soon, we got a communication from the Estée Lauder New York office. Philip Shearer, their Head of Business Development, was visiting India with his team and could we coordinate to meet with them?

We could. We met for dinner at Dum Pukht at the Maurya. Philip was a connoisseur of food and wine, not to mention a racing car enthusiast.

Renee Roen from his team was delightful and loved Indian food. It had all the makings of a great evening, which it was. The only glitch came when Philip ordered the wine because he thought he was paying the bill, which Sam was going to do. He looked at the wine that Philip had ordered and prayed that his credit card would cover it! Philip did not know about the Indian custom of making sure that you took care of the bill before the meal was over if you were entertaining someone, and luckily Sam's credit card did just cover it!

Philip and Renee had obviously met with a lot of other companies as well and had some hilarious stories to tell. Once, they were taken to a room and showed movies of what was meant to showcase the owner's royal lineage. It had obviously been cut from other movies and the heroine kept changing, but they were told it was 'her' in various stages of 'her' life.

They had also done their homework with Forest Essentials, and thought it a great fit with the philosophy of their company. We finished dinner, promised to meet again very soon and came home.

I still remember that evening. We were so charged up—something was happening, we weren't quite sure what, but it was going to be good for the company.

'We have some chilled champagne in the fridge. Shall we celebrate?' Sam said.

'Of course!'

We opened the bottle and poured two glasses.

'Here's to the future, Mom.'

We were in no way prepared for what the future was or would bring but it was going to be effervescent, like the champagne. That we were both convinced about.

————

Sam and I have a complex mother–son relationship, possibly because I had him when I was so young, that we were at some level growing up together. When I look back at the journey of my life, he was my constant companion. The one I used to laugh, fight, be angry with—and also the only one who could put a soothing salve on my wounds. Because of our circumstances, he was also brought up more protectively than most boys his age, which somehow retained his inner core of innocence. He retains it till this day. He has his grandfather's impeccable taste, his father's largesse and a great ability to connect with people at any level.

Over the last few years, I have seen him take more interest in his work, be more painstaking in his execution and more decisive and analytical for the future. This delights me.

Once, many years ago, when he must have been thirteen or fourteen, I bought him a jacket that he really loved. I laboured over whether to buy it or not because it was very expensive. Finally, I gave it, and needless to say he was thrilled. A few months later, I saw a gardener who was wearing something which looked strangely familiar. *'Yeh toh bahut accha lag raha hai, Manoj.'*

'Ji haan. Yeh toh Bhaiya ne diya hai,' the gardener told me.

I was livid. I couldn't believe that Sam had given him the jacket I had paid so much for.

'Where is your new jacket, Samrath? Why are you not wearing it?' I asked Sam.

He looked uncomfortable. 'Actually, Mom, the gardener was shivering, so I took it off and gave it to him.'

I stopped, my anger dissipating.

'May God keep his hand over you, Sam, and allow you to do this always.'

30

A Momentous Year

2008 was a tumultuous year.

One of the first awards for the Soundarya Advanced Age-Defying Serum came at the start of the year. It was quite an accolade for a product that was researched extensively from ancient texts and had been made in the exact manner and with the same ingredients that were intended to be there. The blending of fresh cow's milk with the purest oils, infusions of precious herbs, the twenty-four carat gold-ash bhasma—it was the serum that reportedly was used in Indian mythology by Goddess Lakshmi to retain 'the exquisite texture of her rose-petal skin, which had the glow of a thousand lamps'.

It was yet another time we had attempted to make a product, which had to have not only the finest ingredients but also long and exacting procedures without which it would not have the efficacy that it was intended to.

From the copper vats in which the serum was simmered to the purity of the gold ash, it had to be the same, every time.

It was a time-consuming and very elaborate ritual but if we had decided to take this route, it had to be the real thing—and it was. Awards were just an affirmation. It grew to become one of our bestselling products through the years and we had no PR or advertisements. Everyone who used it recommended it and its popularity spread like wildfire.

It was also the year that Sam met Karishma.

We had wanted him to get married for the last four or five years and it had been an uphill task. Either the girl was not intelligent enough or not pretty enough or too tall or too short for him, the family was not quite right and so on and so forth.

It was an old family friend, Sanjiv Tyagi, who knew both our families and suggested Karishma for Sam. An arranged marriage? Sam was quite sceptical.

'Meeting and going out with girls has not helped,' I said. 'Sometimes these things work best. Why don't you meet her?'

They met for lunch. Her mother and I both waited anxiously to hear how it went. When the lunch did not end soon, I had my first inkling that this may be it.

'Samu, how does it feel?'

'Well, Mom, I can really talk to her. It's really strange. She understands what I am saying and I understand what she is feeling.'

When I met her, I understood what he meant. She was bright, relatively unexposed and very lovely. She had her fundamentals very clear—family came first. That was the way she had been brought up.

It was just what I wanted for Sam. She was young but had her head very firmly grounded.

They got married in March 2008 and Karishma became an integral part of our family. She and I share a relationship other than that of a daughter- and mother-in-law and have shared not only long, intense revelations on life occasionally but also incredibly fun holidays together.

I actually don't remember a time when she was not there!

———

The other major event in 2008 was the signing of a partnership between Forest Essentials and the Estée Lauder companies.

We were invited this time to London to meet with the Estée Lauder team. Sam, our trusted Chartered Accountant Neeraj Puri, and I were to go. Shortly before leaving, I got a call from Abhay. He had been on the board of L'Oréal for many years in India and wanted to meet me.

'Are you home this evening?' he said. 'I have something important to discuss with you.'

'Is everything okay, Yog? I asked, concerned, as he was generally very cool about most things.

'Absolutely fine. Actually, very much so.'

When he came over, he seemed excited. 'I got a call from Jean-Paul Agon this morning. He is the global CEO of L'Oréal, and would like to meet you with regard to Forest Essentials.'

'Okay,' I said slowly. 'Is he here? We are going to London in a few days to meet with the EL team.'

'No, he is in Paris. I told him you are going to meet them, and he wants to know if it is possible to stop in Paris and meet him on the way there.'

'I'm not sure, Yog,' I said, a bit taken aback.

'I don't think you realize what a big deal it is for him to call, Miru. If you like, I will come with you to Paris and you and Sam can stop for a day before you carry on.'

'Okay, Yog.' There was no question of disagreeing with him. We changed our flights.

At the Orly Airport, when we arrived, there was a liveried chauffeur waiting for us with a limousine. We were driven directly to the L'Oréal headquarters a little outside Paris. It was an imposing chateau-like building with a sweeping entrance, set in immaculately landscaped surroundings.

I looked at Sam, who also seemed rather overwhelmed. 'Wow. Quite an office!'

We were led by an attractive dark-haired girl into what seemed like a very large room, with floor-to-ceiling windows on each side, reflecting impossibly perfect flower-laden trees.

The gentleman sitting inside had risen from his desk and was coming towards us. 'Thank you so much for coming. It is an absolute pleasure to meet you,' said this tall, charming man. We were introduced to him by Abhay, and he put us at ease immediately.

'I must tell you, Mira, that my wife has been using Forest Essentials products and loves them. She persuaded me to try your shower gel and I must say I thoroughly enjoyed using it too.'

'I'm so glad to hear that, Mr Agon. That feels very good.' I smiled.

'Would you like to take a look around our R&D facilities? I believe that is what really interests you?'

'Would love to.'

The R&D centre was quite incredible. They seemed to have everything there that anyone could possibly require. I had never seen anything like it.

We came back to his office and spoke about many things. He was interested to know how I had started the business, about Indian culture and how unique India was in terms of being several countries in one. He then said, 'Would you like to go in for lunch?'

There was a smaller private dining room attached to his office where a table was beautifully laid out. His Head of Mergers and Acquisitions joined us, and we sat down to a delicious three-course meal served by his personal chef.

'It is slightly more spicy because I know Indians prefer spicy food,' said this star performer.

'Could not be more perfect, thank you,' I said, completely awed with the style and elegance of the meal.

After lunch, he called me aside. 'We would very much like to partner with you, Mira, and I will see that you get whatever you envisage for the brand. I also know that you are going to meet with Estée Lauder and we are happy to go beyond whatever they may offer you.'

It was a memorable meeting with a charismatic man. In any other circumstances, and if it had not been for my previous meeting with Leonard Lauder, things may have been very different today.

————

2008 was quite a momentous year. Work can sometimes bring you to places that are tailor-made for you; the old Taj in Mumbai was my favourite home away from home. It happened that I used to visit the Taj every few months. It organically developed into a rhythm over time: two nights every five or six months. By then we had five or six stores in Mumbai and I used to personally check the ambience, the training, the quality of service. I never thought to sit up and value the joy of its regular appearance in my life till one ordinary day in 2008.

I had driven straight to the Taj from the Santacruz airport for my regular two-night stay.

It was work as usual. We drew up to the old Taj entrance. In those days it was a separate entrance, on the Gateway of India side of the gorgeous old-world hotel. Pigeons were flying around in the air, looking for the grain that bird lovers threw near the Gateway, gazing over the Arabian Sea. The waves were nondescript, quiet, and cars were whizzing past in a rain of blowing horns. I was looking in my bag for my sunglasses just before stepping out of the car.

At the reception, I relaxed, feeling comfortable. The woodwork friezes and the cool expanses of white on the floor, the efficiency and the quiet charm—yes, home.

That was when I saw the first signs of something different. There were two men checking in right next to me. They wore worn haversacks. I noticed it but it was just that. Nothing more. I remember being struck by the fact that they wore jeans that had seen better days, looked very fit and tightly coiled—just an impression, which I could not describe in any other way. Well, I would not have normally associated them with the regular clientele at the Taj.

A little later, I settled into my room on the sixth floor. I freshened up and left for the work that I had come for. There was a pre-lunch meeting. I stepped out of my room, taking in the quiet of the sixth floor. The carpeted wooden gallery led to the perfectly efficient lifts.

After an entire morning and a part of the afternoon that day, my work was through. Sam was also flying to Mumbai the same evening for some part of the work next morning. I realized that I did not have anything to do now. But my flight was booked for the day after.

Sam was returning a day earlier. The next day. Suddenly, I decided that it was pointless staying for an extra day since my work was over and anyway Sam was booked for the next evening. That was it. I would go back to Delhi with him on his flight.

He joined me for dinner that night with friends in Mumbai. I told him that I was reducing my stay by a day and would be able to return with him. We got my flight preponed.

The next morning, a fateful day for the Taj (and for the world), I woke up to a lovely leisurely day. Later that morning I went to Joy Shoes as usual, to see what was new. I walked around in the shopping arcade, checking out the stores, enjoying the elegance and the lack of rush. Then around 1.30 p.m., Sam and I had soup at the Golden Dragon since we wanted to keep it light. Then we drove to the airport and caught the 5.30 p.m. flight home to Delhi.

By the time we landed in Delhi, the airport was on red alert. Soon, we discovered that all of India was on red alert. Actually, the entire world was! There was chaos at the airport when we stepped out of the plane. A terrorist attack had taken place in Mumbai. The Taj was the epicentre. It had turned into a war zone in those few hours! All the places I had visited that morning within the hotel, even the Golden Dragon, had been destroyed.

The terrorists, I saw on TV, had been on the same floor as me! The sixth! Lives, so many lives, had been lost. Gun battles were raging. India was in mourning, and it seemed to me like war with Pakistan was a real possibility. Friends and relatives were calling us frantically. 'Where are you? Delhi? Thank God!', 'Weren't you supposed to be in Mumbai?', 'Oh my God, oh my God,' 'We are watching it on TV, where were you,' 'You're so lucky—the devil's luck.'

I was in complete shock. I was right there just a few hours earlier. Miraculously, I had not stayed for my usual second night at the Taj. I would always stay there for two nights without exception. Who had changed my mind? Who had made my work get over? I had been sent away ... I had escaped death!

I may have lost my mother to violence, my marriage to violence, my hopes and dreams may have crumbled, my father went before my eyes. But God's hand was over my head through it all. He had always protected me. Always. And here He was again ... That peaceful Paathi who had presided over Papa's Kirtan had been right. I was saved by Him while I was right in the epicentre of India's worst terrorist attack to date.

Maybe my child, Forest Essentials, was not done with me yet.

31

The Start of Realization

Not long after all that, Choti came up to me. I was in my bedroom. Choti and her second husband, Krishna Prasad, now lived on the first floor, the one that I had constructed after Papa's death.

She sat on my bed.

'I have something to tell you.'

'Hmm.' She always had something to tell me. Most of it bad.

'We have sold my share,' Choti said.

'Share? What share?' I felt my stomach coil—it was good at sensing trouble. Enough practice helps.

'My share of this house. Panchsheel. I have sold my share to a builder.'

I thought she was joking.

'What builder?' I said, half joking it off, half scared.

I never relaxed with my sister. Right from the white mouse in my frock from childhood.

'I told you I want to sell, we should sell, we should sell ... you never listen, so ... so now I have done it.'

It was true that Choti would keep saying that we should sell the house.

And I would say, 'No, because it is Papa's house. Our kids can do what they want later.'

'God, Choti!' I was in shock. 'What have you done! You've sold your share?'

This was beyond everything.

'You never paid attention. I told you so many times. It's not my fault. We have sold my share to a broker. He's already given me fifty lakhs as advance.'

'You're mad!' I held my head, feeling a headache coming on.

'Well, I've done it.' Choti shrugged, looking at me rocking to and fro. My brain was numb. I had no idea what to do.

The broker came the next day. He spoke in Hindi and he did not waste time with extra words.

'I'm Mohan. Half this house is mine. We have bought it from your sister and already paid the advance. We will be moving in upstairs in the next few days,' he informed me.

I tried desperately to keep calm. And I began to spin about frantically as well.

I called a lawyer friend and Neeraj, my Chartered Accountant. I consulted with them on how one could go about this whole matter.

Soon after that there was another phone call. Representatives of Estée Lauder.

The Lauders were requesting for a business conference call with Sam and me. Again, I was holding my head in my hands. I was as numb as when Choti had dropped her bomb. Good news. Should we get excited? But a conference call! We didn't have a conference room. I decided to call my friend Shiv to ask how to go about it.

'Shiv, guess what? Estée Lauder has called! But I really need your help because they want to have a conference call with us and we don't have a conference room.'

Shiv said he would give us the conference room in his office for the call.

On the appointed day and at the appointed time, we spoke to the representatives of Estée Lauder.

They had loved our work, they said, and wanted to buy a twenty per cent share in our company. They offered us an advance of what seemed a large sum of money, at the time. I could not even work out what that was. I had not even thought such a momentous event in our lives would happen just like that. But for that matter, I never doubted our potential either.

On the other hand, I had never thought that a property broker called Mohan would walk into my house one fine day and inform me that half the house was his.

But all this aside, the fact was that Mohan needed to be bought out as fast as possible, to get rid of him.

I called my friend Bindu and said, 'You are not going to believe what has happened!'

'You are sounding very stressed, Mira, come over immediately and let's discuss it,' she said. I went with Sam, as he was also close to her, and we told her the whole incident. I still remember her advice to Sam, 'Don't let them do anything to jeopardize the house, Samu. I know what your mother has done to save it. You have to do the same.'

I did not have the kind of money required to save the house from any angle at all. Necessity is the mother of invention, they say, and sure enough, Sam came up with an ingenious idea.

'We have no choice. You will have to develop Panchsheel, much as you hate the fact. Let's talk to a developer, give Masi her money and get two flats made. Bobo is the answer, Mom.'

'Bobo? Your friend?' I couldn't understand. Sam spelt it out.

'Bobo's mom has a construction company as well, and they handle property. At least it's better to go to people you know and can trust instead of some constructor.'

'That's true,' I said. I knew Bobo was a close friend of Sam's, and he was very fond of him.

I didn't really know Kuki Chowdhary, Bobo's mother. I had heard that she was a wealthy woman with a keen business acumen.

A meeting was worked out. Sam and I went to meet Kuki. She invited us to her office. Not home. It did strike a slightly jarring note, but as usual, I did not pause and listen to that whisper in my head. *I could understand*, I said to myself.

After all, this was not about Bobo being Sam's friend. This was going to involve business. Office, not home, was fine.

Kuki was very cordial during that initial meeting.

I explained the bind that I was in with Choti, the broker and my arrangement with Estée Lauder, which could not come through in time to get rid of Mohan. Kuki said it would all become better and offered to give me the money straightaway.

It would solve my problem immediately. She said that I would have to sign all the papers, which were just formalities. Then the property would be rebuilt into four flats, with two flats for us and the other two for her.

I worked out that this way we would get to keep Papa's property, give Choti what she wanted desperately and still have our own apartment, one for myself and one for the children. It sounded like the only way out.

So, I just went ahead. There were not too many choices. She gave me one crore that day as an advance.

The very next day, I gave Mohan the broker one crore, which was double his advance, and with that I managed to get rid of him.

Now there was Choti left to deal with. I was sure I would find a way of giving her the monetary value that she wanted for her share in Papa's property too, without losing the property in my lifetime.

At first, I did not realize that I had got myself into the wrong situation—a situation that was not really designed in my interest—but by then it was too late.

The deal with Choti was still not done—we had only paid the broker but did not have the money to pay the rest. Also, Kuki's collaboration had not worked out eventually, because of which we could not accept any money from her. Therefore, the money from the US came at an opportune time.

It was the strangest thing. I had never thought of selling any part of Forest Essentials and had to do it with really no choice—to pay my sister for her share of our joint property!

The whole cheque went to her. We bought an apartment that she wanted in Panchsheel Park and put in a substantial amount for Jai, her son, as a gift.

She showed the sale in her income tax papers, got a tax waiver for her new apartment and things seemed to have settled quite nicely as she started doing up her new home.

There was still some amount pending which was to be paid to her, which I said would take a year for us to clear.

My sister, who was handling her own money for the first time, said, 'That's fine. You will have to pay interest on the remaining money. I will leave the house papers with Neeraj and when you make the full payment, he can give you the papers.'

I was speechless. 'Yes,' I said, in disbelief.

That was fine. Of course, she was entirely within her rights to do so.

I thought of the nightmare years after Papa died leaving no will, month after month, going to courts, getting paperwork done, affidavits, notices, all to get the will divided clearly and equally in both our names.

I thought of her, so unwell, so vulnerable always, and that I had to take care of her, that there was no one else.

That memory made me smile—a little tremulously perhaps—but smile I did.

The next one year, Sam and I both put in our salaries into making the monthly payments, after which very little was left over for us. Sam was not very happy, but I said that there was no other way of doing this.

'Didn't even want to buy the house, Mom,' he said wearily.

'Well, there's no choice, Samu. I promise you there will be days when money won't be a problem.'

He looked a bit disbelieving but said nothing.

It did happen. The last payment was finally made. The papers were signed and the property deeds given to us. It seemed a hollow victory.

32

Soundarya Day Cream

We began experimenting with a night cream, infusing the popular Soundarya Serum in it.

The gold base was brilliant. Gold is a metal that the skin absorbs easily. It improves elasticity and it has age-defying properties. It protects the skin from the sun and from the damaging effects of pollution in the environment. But for Soundarya as a night cream, we were confronted with one difficulty after the other. The serum made the cream too heavy—reducing the serum kept the texture lighter but reduced its benefits! It had to be the perfect blend to have optimal richness yet easily permeate the skin. Its colour and fragrance had to be light and delicate. It was not yet absolutely perfect.

We kept going up and down from Rishikesh to Lodsi to Delhi to Rishikesh to Lodsi to Delhi, struggling with nuances of texture and finish.

Finally, one morning, we got it just right. It was a Eureka moment—although there was a slight concern that it may still be lighter than a heavy-duty night cream—but it was a brilliant product. The whole team had been working on it for months and there was a sense of relief and then celebration in the air. By now, our regulatory celebration fare was samosa–kachori and a sweet ghee speciality from Rishikesh. We all celebrated, knowing that this was going to be special. We then had the packaging in place, the quality tests done, the cream filled in the jars, ready for dispatch. I called a meeting.

'I want to discuss the details of the new Soundarya Night Cream and the plans for the launch.'

The team was listening. I was talking when Jaqueline, our amazingly competent Regional Manager and now Head—National Retail, said, 'Won't this kill our Date and Litchi, ma'am?'

'Yes, you are right. It probably will.' Jaq with her unerring intuition was absolutely right. She was, and always has been, such an important part of the evolution of Forest Essentials.

And suddenly I knew this was all wrong. The Date and Litchi Cream was doing so well as a night cream. How could we suffocate it by giving it competition from Soundarya? But what were we to do with the fabulous Soundarya Night Cream? Then it came to me:

'Wait!' I said. 'Soundarya can't be a *night* cream. It's also light for a night cream but perfect for the day.'

Everyone looked taken aback.

'Soundarya will be a *day* cream.'

'How? It's already done. We are ready to dispatch to the stores in the next week.'

'Gold is great for skin protection from sun damage and pollution, the texture is perfect, and it plumps and protects the skin … so we just have to do what we can to make it a day cream.'

'But … how?'

I was adamant. And the answers began to appear. We added Yasadh Bhasma, a natural zinc extract, to it for sun protection and it was born that day.

A cream that went straight to the top of our bestseller list and has remained there ever since.

33

Realization

It was the first of January 2012. There was an official-looking court notice which was lying on the table when I came out of my room.

I picked it up and opened the stiff envelope. It was full of endless legal jargon until I stopped. 'Anuradha Prasad files a case stating she has not sold her property at Panchsheel Park and her signatures were taken under duress.'

The paper was shaking in my hand. I sat down in the chair, trembling. It could not be possible. I must have read something wrong.

I sent a message to Sam and Karishma to come down urgently and they ran down in their pyjamas.

'What's the matter? Are you okay?'

I gestured towards the papers. 'Just read these. I think I'm hallucinating.'

Karishma started reading. Her face got whiter and Sam was curiously immobile.

It was true. Choti had filed a case against me, saying that I had cheated her of her share of the property. Of course, in my foolish naivete, I had not registered the sale deed. I just thought I would do it when it was necessary.

It was one of those moments when you can see something happening but you feel it's not happening to you. I kept thinking that any moment someone was going to say, 'Fooled you! It's a joke!'

But, of course, it was not a joke. What she had written was unbelievable—she was forced to sell, she never wanted to sell the property, her signatures were taken under duress, she was advised wrongly and so on.

So endlessly on.

I called Diviya. She had already heard from her brother and sister-in-law and rushed over. I picked up the document and gave it to her and she started reading it in shock.

'It's not true, Mom. There has to be some mistake. This must be Krishna Prasad forcing her. Masi could never do this.' She was in tears, unable to believe that her Masi, with whom she had had a very close bond since childhood, could have actually done this.

However, we had to respond to the letter—speak to a lawyer, do whatever had to be done.

The lawyer again was astounded. 'Who could have possibly advised her to do this? She has taken the money, taken exemption in income tax, written receipts over two years and been paid interest!'

Well, it was what it was.

What the case has made me realize is that going to court is an exercise where no one really cares what the truth is. It's just how it's presented. No one really wins except the lawyers.

It was a sad end to a lifelong relationship, and it hurt for the longest time. Probably the saddest thing was that she would eventually be the biggest loser. Losing out on her only family. By the time Choti would realize that, it would be too late.

34

In the World's Gaze

We had always had the greater vision of being the foremost brand in Luxury Ayurveda in India and then taking it global. This meant that we would be on display in the international landscape. Around that time, I had stepped back for a review because I sensed that our direction was somehow askew.

What was not right? I wondered. Our look was simple, minimal. Our colour palette was pastel. Our fonts were clean. The problem was not clear.

We had customer research conducted to get a better view. And voila! the culprit appeared.

It showed us that we were being seen as a Western brand because India did not have any beauty brands in the highly premium segment. For me this was an identity issue—our identity was Indian and luxury, not Western and luxury.

It had become crucial to look Indian. But how were we to express this identity? We fell feverishly into this project. By the time 2009 came, we made a huge shift in our brand image towards a clearly Indian tilt. It was drastic. It was risky. We had been recognized in a certain manner and now we were dropping that look.

Forest Essentials appeared in its new persona by 2010. We were dramatically different from our earlier look. But we were in harmony with our DNA. Our colours were now jewel tones. The look was rich. Our products appeared hand-drawn on the labels, in the style of Mughal miniatures.

Mr Lauder personally took an interest in overseeing the logo, which went from a simple tree to a more complex Tree of Life. Beautifully etched, you can actually see a glimpse of Lord Ganesha if you look closely. That, to us, was quite incredible! And, of course, suitably auspicious.

———

It seems the right time to talk about Daniel.

Much earlier, at the time that we were looking to sign the contract, I got a call from Mr Lauder while I was in Rishikesh to say that Philip Shearer would be exiting the company, and because he knew that we had shared a great rapport with him, he wanted to bring it up before I heard it from someone else.

I was a little shaken with the news.

With his extraordinary sensitivity, Mr Lauder had asked William, his son, to meet Sam and me for lunch to meet with Daniel Rachmanis. We met in London at Nobu, a fashionable restaurant in Park Lane renowned for its Japanese food. I was determined to dislike anyone who had come in Philip's place and I think Sam was more excited about the food!

We met with William, who very graciously introduced us to Daniel— he seemed much nicer than I had expected and our talks continued.

Little did we know that in the years to come, Daniel would become not only a valued business partner but also a very dear friend. He has contributed greatly to Forest Essentials, helping it reach where it is today, and has been very instrumental in keeping a balance between our point of view of what would work for an Indian brand and how this would translate to someone from a Western culture.

Now Forest Essentials had colours like gold, teal blue, luminescent red and saffron yellow. The market responded warmly to India and luxury. Each label carried detailed explanations. We had Lord Hanuman, for example, on the label for our Advanced Sanjeevani Beauty Elixir.

In the great epic, the Ramayana, the story goes that Lord Hanuman went to look for the Sanjeevani herb to save Lord Lakshman's life. When he could not find it, in desperation, he carried back the entire mountain where it was supposed to be growing! It was known as an incredibly rejuvenating herb, or 'one that could bring back life'. The Sanjeevani herb that he was fabled to have found grew on the higher slopes of the Himalayas, and was infused in our pre-moisturizer.

It was in 2009 that the awards had started coming in for products, for the brand and unexpectedly even for me!

I never worked for awards, so being noticed was like being woken up from an enjoyable reverie to this strange sensation called 'recognition'. I began to be shown where 'we' were appearing in newspapers and magazines of the world—*Elle*, *Vogue*, *Grazia*, *GQ*, *Economic Times*, with Estée Lauder, Lancôme and Clinique. Media attention was great for the brand but personally something I never enjoyed.

While the Haridwar factory got formal credibility with a GMP pharmaceutical-grade certification, our Noida office seemed to be shrinking in size compared to Forest Essentials' growing needs. We left that space and moved into a new bigger office in the same area.

We still operate from that Noida office; only now we occupy the whole building because there has to be enough space.

In the meantime, the awards continued—*Harper's Bazaar, Vogue, Economic Times* and so on. In the same year, we opened our first travel retail store in Mumbai's international airport. Today, we have stores in all the major airports in India.

Competition was beginning to appear. Our products and look were constantly being copied. Suddenly, everyone was into Ayurveda!

'Let it happen,' I used to say to my outraged team. 'It is a sign that we must move ahead. Copying and competing are good signs. It means we are popular.'

35

The Break-in

It was sometime around the end of 2010, in late November or early December. We had just gone through the usual night routine. We finished dinner, the servants went around locking the doors and I went into my bedroom.

My handbag was on the chair in my bedroom and it had some notes that I had been working on that day. I took out the manuscript and sat in bed for a while, completing those notes. I must have gone to sleep at around 10.45 or eleven p.m.

Suddenly, sometime around two in the morning, I was awakened by a sound—was it a brush against something? I have always been a very light sleeper. It seemed like there was someone in my room. I got up with my heart beating faster and asked, *'Kaun hai?'* There was no answer. Maybe I was mistaken. However, I had had the distinct feeling that there was someone standing near the foot of my bed. By now I was terrified. I switched on the lights and got out of bed. There was no one.

My door was unlocked. I opened it slightly and said, 'Is anyone there?' No answer. There was complete darkness, but I thought I could feel the presence of someone. I closed the door with my hands shaking slightly and locked it. I remember trying to tell myself that I was letting my imagination go haywire, and went back to bed and kept all the lights on. Imagination or not, it was very frightening. I found it difficult to even close my eyes. However, I must have eventually fallen asleep.

The next morning, I heard loud knocking on my door and when I opened it, Karishma and then Sam and then our old cook Sultan rushed in, looking at me in disbelief.

They were all dishevelled and agitated and kept saying, 'Are you okay? Thank God you're okay.'

'What is the matter with all of you? I am fine,' I said.

'Come out,' said Karishma, and led me to the drawing room. The handbag, which had been in my room, was thrown open and its contents scattered over the sofa. Unable to comprehend, I sank into a chair. Everyone was quiet and in shock.

This is what Sultan had seen at 6.30 in the morning when he came into the house, and he had rushed up to call the children.

Again, Sultan shouted, *'Hey Bhagwan, yeh kya hua!'* And we all rushed into the kitchen. He stood shaking. There were two kitchen knives, which had been taken out of their wooden stand and were gleaming on the kitchen counter.

We found out later that someone had entered the Mandir as well, which was just outside my bedroom door, as some things were not in their usual place. It looked like someone had entered and stood inside in front of the Gods, as everything had been shifted to one side. It was clear that somebody or some people had entered the house, gone into the kitchen, the Mandir and then my bedroom, and for some unfathomable reason, only taken my bag and left.

What was still not clear was since the knives were clearly intended for a certain purpose, why had they not been used? Was it maybe because they had entered the Mandir? Was that possible? Well, as strange as the sequence was, it was again another instance of being saved by an unforeseen force, which even today I am unable to define or understand, as always, but am just grateful for.

After this incident, we had the walls of the house raised, additional guards, more security and, of course, I have never left my bedroom door unlocked since.

36

Shabad and Angad

It was 2011—the year Shabad was born. When I went to the hospital, Karishma was already in labour. Finally, we heard the wonderful news—the mother is fine and it's a beautiful baby boy. We were overjoyed.

It was momentous for all of us—Sam, Karishma, her mother and me.

Before that, for many months, many names had been contemplated for boys and girls. The one I immediately loved in their shortlisted ones was Shabad.

It was unusual and it was also, as Samrath's name was, from the Guru Granth Sahib. In the hospital, the baby's birth certificate had to be made, so the name needed to be finalized. Sam and Karishma were in discussion—she also had another name that perhaps her grandmother liked, and Sam was going back and forth.

Finally, I couldn't take it any more. I got up, kissed the baby and said, 'Bye, Shabad. I'm leaving and that's what I'm going to call him. When you both decide on whatever you want, then put it on the certificate.'

Anyway, Shabad it was. The most delightful and happy baby in the world. The joy of all our lives. I have enjoyed him so much while he has been growing up. In so many ways a carbon copy of his father. He has been on many trips with me, from when he was as young as three years old. Loving new places, enjoying new foods, inquisitive about everything and knowledgeable beyond his years.

And then came Angad in 2014. He came into a household where he had an adored older brother. However, his brother, thankfully, loved him straightaway.

Little Angad has made his presence felt. He has a distinct personality and wins hearts with a disarming smile. 'An awesome twosome', as somebody remarked the other day.

Of course, now that they are older, Shabad disdainfully tolerates his younger brother and Angad cannot think of anything beyond him.

37

Floods in Rishikesh

It was 2013. I had gone up to Rishikesh where we were renovating one of the earlier buildings on the land. Tek Singh had joined me and I said to him one evening, 'Why don't we go down to the town? We haven't been for so long, and it would be interesting to see how it is now.'

So, we drove down that evening to Haridwar, went to attend the Aarti and browsed around in the small shops, finding so many new things there and so many more visitors. Many foreigners. We went to the old bookshops on the side of the river.

When we were leaving, I happened to see a beautiful bronze statue of Lord Ganesha in one of the store windows.

'I love it, Tek Singh, it would be lovely for the children upstairs, they don't have a Ganeshji.'

I went to the store and spoke to the shopkeeper. He quoted a very high price, so I left it and said no. Walking back, I said to Tek Singh, 'I really liked it but the shopkeeper was asking for too much.'

'*Agar itna achha laga, ma'am, aapko le lena chahiye. Hai bahut hi sunder,*' he said.

I went back. The shopkeeper saw me coming in and smiled.

'You have made a very good choice, madam,' he said. 'It is a very unique and lucky Ganeshji for the house that it's in.'

'I'm getting it for my son and daughter-in-law,' I said.

'In that case, I will give it to you for a little less.'

I thanked him and carried it back to the car.

The next morning we were leaving for Delhi, so I kept the Ganeshji in my room for the night. In the morning, I packed and left for the airport to catch the flight.

At about six in the evening, I started getting frantic calls—the water level of the river was rising frighteningly high. The next morning the river had swept everything in its path. The shops on both sides of the river had been submerged under the powerful sweep of the Ganga. There was torrential rain.

Roads were swept away, cars, people, animals. Trees were uprooted. Water had come up to the level of the house and the ground floor had water till the ceiling. Our temple was under water.

The shop where I had bought the Ganeshji statue a day before no longer existed.

I had left on the morning of the floods.

38

As We Go On

In the meantime, Forest Essentials was going from strength to strength.

Festive gifting became a hallmark of Forest Essentials as we introduced a new thematic collection once a year in September at the onset of the festive season. Our boxes with their precious contents came wrapped in fragrant tissue, lavishly tied with matching grossgrain ribbons. Beautifully intricate Indian motifs decorated these boxes, making them the perfect gift or just the perfect indulgence.

Packaging has always been a large part of our ethos and it reflects the identity of the brand.

In 2017, *Vogue* was celebrating its tenth anniversary in India. For this special occasion, they wanted to collaborate with a brand that best symbolized India. We worked on the concept to make a unique, unusual product, produced in a traditional manner. The Madhumalti solid perfume was conceptualized in a sophisticated gold compact box, specially for *Vogue*, artisanally made, using the ancient enfleurage method, which is very labour intensive. Scented flowers were soaked in a blend of natural butters and oils every day, removed and replaced with fresh flowers for at least four weeks to encapsulate their exquisite fragrance.

The perfume was called Blend No. 10, as a tribute to ten years of *Vogue* in India.

Huffington Post USA covered the Forest Essentials journey in an exclusive in-depth story feature about Indian beauty rituals, imbibing Ayurvedic principles and the phenomenal rise of natural beauty products.

It was also this year that I was awarded the Beauty Pioneer of the Year by *Vogue* India.

———

Various things were happening one after the other, and we decided to redesign the stores with a global design agency to reflect the brand in India and internationally.

The design had elements of an authentic Ayurvedic workspace with its key ingredients, including pure hand-pressed oils, taking pride of place. The map of India in the store showcases the roots of the brand and its proud Indian lineage.

A very interesting new concept was introduced by Forest Essentials in 2017 using original herbal decoctions, or Kashyams, prescribed in ancient Vedic texts, into the country's first Ayurvedic Sheet Masks. Made with organic cotton cellulose, three variants—Ojas, Tejasvi and Sundari—were launched, each addressing a specific skin concern. The Masks got a great response.

———

In 2017, we also expanded our Haridwar factory to include the next-door premises, and to mirror the current establishment. The talks carried on for about four months. The market rate was lower than what the owner was asking for and he refused to negotiate, knowing how crucial it was for us to expand. It was a stalemate. Finally, on a visit to the factory, I said to our Manager that we needed this more and so we must be ready to pay a higher price. 'Take this offer to him and close the deal. Say, "This is it or we will buy something else."' It was also a lesson. When you actually want something, its price becomes immaterial.

The deal was finally closed and we were able to double our capacity without much additional outlay. The factory is now a world-class manufacturing facility, with pharmaceutical-grade production standards.

———

In 2014, India became the first country in the world to legally mandate corporate social responsibility or CSR, making it imperative for companies of a certain turnover and profitability to compulsorily spend two per cent of their average net profit on CSR initiatives.

This included education, health, gender equality, women empowerment, skill-training and social-enterprise projects. For us, this was actually a validation of our already existing practices of women empowerment, primary rural education and skill-training.

The Niti Aayog, the country's premier policymaking institution, provides directives and technical services that include all the CSR initiatives. Their team does a stellar job with their CEO, Amitabh Kant.

In 2017, I was also appointed a mentor for the Aayog Women's Entrepreneurial Platform, or the WEP, a prestigious assignment, which has fostered many a talented woman entrepreneur across the country and shows a promising road ahead.

39

Acquisition

In 2017, I happened to have a chance conversation with someone at the factory. I was discussing whether any land was available with a water source, as that was a problem in the Uttarakhand villages. Although we had spring water on our own Rishikesh land, I was looking at something where we could eventually bottle the water, as this terrain had pure mineral-rich water from Himalayan springs.

Interestingly, he spoke of an area near his own village where they had a pure spring water source on the land, but he said that it was impossible to acquire, as the land was occupied by seventeen or eighteen families. I discovered that the land was not even ten kilometres away from us!

I came back and discussed it with Tek Singh, my trusted Man Friday, and said that we must try and get this land. I had no idea how we would. Trying to deal with one buyer was bad enough but trying to deal with eighteen seemed completely out of the question. He thought about it as he generally did not question me on most things, many of which must have seemed completely incomprehensible to him! As usual, he went directly to the root of the problem. He said, 'We need to see who the key people are, who other people will listen to.'

He eventually identified the key people and for over four or five months, we spoke to them. I spoke to the first two people myself and explained why it would be better for them to have their own homes as opposed to more communal living where everyone had a stake in everyone else's property, which they also agreed was giving rise to many internal issues and inevitable family infighting.

Eventually, instead of just offering them money, we bought plots of alternate land for them on which they could then build their own homes. Initially, they could not give us any papers because the lands and their ownership was entwined with too many families. This was a move that might have not worked had they taken the land and not helped us with the rest of the acquisition, but it was a chance, and I said that we must take it because there was no other way of ever being able to acquire this.

It really was a large gamble because the other sixteen families were adamant about not selling. Convincing them seemed a distant possibility.

However, it is providential that after these two people got their own lands, they helped advise other families and convince them of the fact that it was better to get an independent piece of land rather than one where all had multiple family interests. It took time and patience, which is something I personally found very difficult.

The last and most difficult hurdle was a woman who was widowed and owned the maximum amount of land. She said she would not go as it was her husband's land and completely resisted every effort from our side to speak with her, or any of our attempts to explain.

Finally, I called and met with her, and said that we were going to build something on the land where her husband had lived, which he would be very proud of. Instead of her staying alone on a tract of land, where anyone could walk through because the surrounding land had been sold, we could get her a home which we would have built for her, and she would be secure.

She listened and then said regally that she would think about it. I appreciated her dignity and said she should let me know whenever she had decided what she wanted to do. A month later, she sent a message, and I went to meet with her.

She held my hand and said, 'I believe that you will do it but first make sure that you get me a place where I am independent and I am not dependent on my sons, since I don't trust my daughters-in-law!' I promised her and we got some land that she approved of, and had a small house built for her on it.

She was delighted!

She was the final one who sold, and more importantly gave me her blessings, because she said I had been more of a son to my father than a daughter.

I told her she simply had to see her own strength to know there was no disparity between men and women.

———

Then, sometime in early 2018, I came to know of some land that was for sale near our factory in Lodsi. Land rarely came up for sale in that area. I went to see it because I thought buying something there would be useful for us at some point in the future.

This land was on top of a hill. It was a bit of a plateau and the top was completely rocky. It was like a solid sheet of rock when I first saw it. However, I was astounded by the view and its position where it overlooked three quarters of the valley.

I had gone with Tek Singh and when we got out of the car, both of us looked down at this land, which seemed completely unapproachable.

Tek Singh said, 'We can't even reach it and building a road is going to be impossible, so let us not even attempt this. *Abhi samajh aaya kyun bik raha hai.*' I still didn't want to just leave, so after looking around, we managed to find a small opening hidden by bushes. We went down a kind of sheer ravine-like path and finally went through the dense undergrowth and steep slopes. It seemed like a bizarre obstacle race for which I was clearly unsuited, and by now my initial enthusiasm had abated considerably. By the time we reached flat ground, it was nearing sunset and both of us stopped in silence. The view was incredible. It was just right.

Tek Singh, by now used to this, said he would talk to the owners. Despite the fact that it was for sale, it belonged to two brothers, out of which one was keen to sell and the other not. They kept negotiating and whenever we would reach a consensus, one of them kept raising the price. Finally, I said after the third impasse that it was enough, we were walking away from this. We told them we were not interested. The next morning, they came back to us and we finally managed to close the deal.

I'm told that after we bought the land, the prices shot up! It took us many months and several bulldozers that broke down to level the land and build a road, but we were finally able to reach the flat land with a car! At that time, Sam suggested we get an architect on board and he found us a well-known architectural firm called Morphogenesis.

I was not sure what exactly we were going to do with the new factory, but I knew it was going to be a stunning location if built the way I had envisioned. So, the project started getting built slowly and in a way that I had never experienced before—with meticulous attention and utilizing the experience of the professionals we had taken on board.

This was almost halfway done when we came towards the end of 2019. The factory was getting built with rainwater harvesting and solar heating. It included ducting for air conditioning and heating, stringent measures to make it microbe-free and many features, which made the building state of the art. At this time, I decided that it was also finally time to do a renovation of the Rishikesh property.

40

Diviya's Home

In 2019, I got the opportunity to do something I had always wanted for Diviya since she had got married. Once, in an unguarded moment, she had asked me, if I ever could, to get her an apartment of her own. She normally never asked for anything all these years.

I had also started spending more time with her daughters, now growing up quite rapidly—Rhea into a beautiful young lady about to go to college, and Samaira, a bright creative girl just entering her teens. It always weighed on my mind that I was unable to do much for Diviya when she got married—so that year, we told a few brokers what we were looking for.

Six or seven months passed, and whatever I had seen was just not suitable. Either too ornate and over the top, or too many bedrooms, not enough bedrooms, no sunshine, kitchen too small, no view and so on and so forth.

It went on and on—every weekend or whenever there was time to look, we did. After a while I was fed up. Then one Sunday morning, I got a call that there was one apartment that they thought I would like, since apparently the broker had now realized the parameters that I was looking for!

I thought, *Let's just get it over with.* We drove to where we were supposed to see this apartment and as we came closer, went through a wide avenue towards Vasant Vihar. We then turned into another wide road shaded with large trees and stopped in front of a newly built block, three storeys high.

The entrance had well-marked-out car parking areas. *It's been good so far*, I thought. *Now the apartment itself is going to have something seriously wrong.*

I knew when I walked into the apartment that this was it. The living room overlooked a lush green park where no one could build in the future. It had a beautifully appointed kitchen, and three bedrooms thoughtfully laid out with minute attention to detail.

Finally satisfied, we arranged to meet with the builder and Sam came with me. He was a well-known builder and obviously very experienced with negotiation. When we inquired about the price, I realized it was much more than I had expected to spend. I said so, and he said he had another ready buyer if it was too expensive.

I also realized later that he had probably expected me to ask him to bring it down, but I didn't. I said okay to him and thought I could see a glimpse of surprise, as he must have been getting ready to haggle! When we left, Sam said, 'Mom, don't you think you could have brought it down a little?'

'I suppose we could have, Sam, but I loved it and didn't want to lose it.'

'Okay, he could have made that out from your face anyway!' Sam smiled.

So the deed was done.

Now what remained was letting Diviya and Hitesh know.

The following week, we were all going out to a family lunch. We were leaving the house together since we had all met at home, and I said I would go in Hitesh's car with them to the restaurant. Everyone got into their respective cars and left for the lunch.

On the way, I asked if we could stop at Vasant Vihar for five minutes and read out the address. When we reached there, I said, 'Just come up with me, I don't want to go up alone.' So both of them got out of the car, and we went up in a small immaculate lift to the second floor. The door was open, and we walked in.

'Lovely flat,' said Diviya. 'Whose is it, Ma?'

'Just had to have a look at it for someone,' I said.

'Wow! What an amazing view,' said Hitesh, going to the balcony. 'Who does it belong to?'

I then took out the envelope with the note I had written to them, along with the keys of the house, and gave it to Diviya, who looked at it, puzzled.

'What is this, Ma?'

'Just take it into the next room and open it together.'

They were now looking at me in bewilderment but went ahead.

I looked out at the lush gardens and could feel ST's presence there. He seemed to be smiling.

'Oh my God, what is this? What did you do? When? Love it, Mom! Can't believe it!' They both came out with tears running down their cheeks.

'A belated wedding gift, Diviya, from your father and me.'

They were both overwhelmed and I had finally made peace with myself, with something that had eluded me for many years.

Everyone else at the lunch had known beforehand and there was much celebration, tears and joy.

This was also the time that I actually got to know Hitesh well as a person, after so many years. He is fairly reserved but as he opens up, there is an extremely fun-loving side of his personality. He is deeply caring and considerate. We have had some memorable times together as a family.

41

Recognition

Our new e-commerce website was redesigned by the Bureau of Visual Affairs in London, a digital agency that specializes in content and utility-driven user experiences. They had previously worked with the Tate, the Victoria and Albert Museum, and Jo Malone.

We had a special new launch in 2019. It was a formulation we had worked on for a long time, infused with an intricate, labour-intensive Ayurvedic serum, which took months to prepare.

Called the Ojas Glow Replenishing Beauty Balm, this worked like an 'activator' to enhance the efficacy of night cream. It got absorbed immediately, while illuminating, smoothing and repairing the skin when resting at night.

The Ojas took no time in becoming a 'hero' product. The great thing with this was that we were able to use this serum in many products subsequently, for its almost miraculous performance.

This year saw many recognitions, including Forest Essentials being ranked as one of India's fastest-growing companies by the *Economic Times* and Statista. It was also listed amongst the Financial Times' High-Growth Companies in the Asia-Pacific region. They included us when they introduced *FT 1000*, a special report on innovative high-growth companies as the driving force of the Asia-Pacific economy in the twenty-first century.

It was also an honour to be awarded the ETPrime Women Leadership Award for Businesswoman of the Year in 2019.

Cognizant of the need for effective solutions to reduce plastic waste in the context of growing environmental challenges, we had been strengthening policies towards eco-friendly packaging and organized recycling by partnering with Reliance Industries Ltd (RIL), one of the global leaders in the PET (polyethylene terephthalate) manufacturing space. RIL undertook recycling of waste plastic packaging of Forest Essentials products and converted the plastic into high-quality eco-friendly material.

Many years ago, we had started a unique service enabling our customers to customize their own creams, understanding the importance of personalization. Then, we were perhaps ahead of our time! Over the years, we were actually requested to bring this service back but because of the many difficulties of this high level of personalization, we could not do this for many years.

However, we recognized the unique niche that this could fill and restarted this bespoke service in 2019. It is not a large part of our business but it does what we intended it to, which is cater to people who need something suited to their individual needs, some of which are quite extreme. This service is highly appreciated by people who now only use their own prescription creams created for them.

42

The Start of Another Decade

After pioneering the epitome of luxury and sophistication in holistic beauty for over two decades, Forest Essentials introduced an extension of skincare to accentuate natural beauty. This artisanal collection was inspired from age-old rituals from times where make-up was a concept not to mask or cover, but tint and accentuate. It was also a time which we felt was appropriate to launch a 'feel-good' collection.

Strangely, it was on a trip to New York three years ago that the idea germinated. When having lunch with Leonard Lauder, he brought up what was next: 'Why don't you look at natural make-up?'

'Mr Lauder, we do skincare, how can we venture into make-up? It's a completely different vertical.'

'Try it, Mira. You don't have to continue if it doesn't work.'

He was, with his always impeccable sense of timing, absolutely right.

The new collection included a Gulaab Khaas Kajal made with a rose-petal formula in diyas with wicks soaked in pure ghee the old-fashioned way. The Madhu Rasa Lip Serums were tinted with natural colours like beetroot, pomegranate and jamun berries. The Som Rasa Skin Tints would blur skin to perfection and Cheek Tints provided a wash of blush. The Nayantara Lash and Brow Serum was to nourish as well as keep lashes and brows glossy.

It was an experimental collection but it keeps getting sold out, confirming both the fact that this is what is needed today and also that since it is not made in assembly lines, it's fine to be out of stock!

———

One day while I was in office, I got a call on my mobile.

'Is that Mrs Kulkarni? May I connect you to the Rashtrapati Bhavan?' The gentleman on the other side asked for my address and said that he was sending me an invitation for a dinner in honour of Donald Trump, the US President at the time, who was in India on a visit.

After giving the address, I put the phone down and took a deep breath. I thought about how I should tell this to the children—should I just be cool and say, 'By the way, I won't be home for dinner next Saturday.'

'Oh, where are you going?'

That would be my cue to say casually, 'Well, actually, to the Rashtrapati Bhavan, for dinner with Mr Trump.'

Of course, it didn't really happen like that, as I told them excitedly, 'You are not going to believe this—'

The evening was quite intimidating in the beginning as I didn't know anyone, but luckily I met the daughter and son-in-law of my friends Adita and Sanjay. By now, I had a number of people whom I recognized but did not know, who came up and said wonderful things about Forest Essentials. That felt very good.

Finally, being introduced to the American President and the Prime Minister of India was the sequel to a fairly surreal evening.

43

Renovation

We spoke to Morphogenesis again and they gave us a plan, which was to redesign the original buildings of the Rishikesh property and make them more modern and contemporary. Although when we went through this plan on paper, I could not envisage the details that were captured but saw the renovation more conceptually.

The property was being run by Neemrana hotels and I requested them to give us one building at a time, so that we could do the renovation. We went through a lot of back and forth as they were not completely in favour of this but we started with one block, and entered into March 2020.

I was visiting Rishikesh for a few days around 18 March and there were imminent rumours of a nationwide lockdown because of a new strain of coronavirus. Our close friends Tim and Val were visiting from London and had spent a week with us. They were in the South when it seemed that there would be an embargo on flights going out. Suddenly everyone wanted to get home and most people were in panic as there were no tickets available. Luckily, Sam pulled a few strings and was able to get them the last few tickets for going back to London. He has since been their favourite nephew!

Two days later, without any warning, a nationwide lockdown was announced. One by one all our stores were closing, most businesses were impacted including hospitality and airlines, and as a consequence, restaurants and leisure businesses as well. Construction companies were amongst those severely disabled, as most of the migrant workers could not be paid and they had started moving back to their villages.

During these exceptionally challenging times, as a socially conscious beauty company, we tried to make our resources and facilities available to help the surrounding communities. Hygiene was a mainstay in the absence of a vaccine or effective antiviral drugs. Since the factories were closed for regular business, we manufactured high-quality sanitizers, surface cleansers and soaps, which were distributed in Uttarakhand to the police forces, hospitals and frontline workers, to assist in any way we could. We sent supplies to Delhi when trucks could ply to aid the immense efforts of many hospitals including AIIMS, Apollo and Lok Nayak. It was a collective effort with everyone doing what they could to help in whichever way possible.

In Rishikesh, I saw the lockdown as an opportunity to complete the renovation.

'What is the need to renovate, Mira? The property is fine,' said the management at the Neemrana hotels.

'But I will do everything and this lockdown is the best time to do it. Please let us do this.'

They were not in favour of the total renovation as they thought people would still visit the hotel. We had time till March 2021, when their lease ended, so I was left with little choice.

There was no way to leave Rishikesh and no one was clear about how long this would last. I actually ended up staying there for eight months. There were already some labourers on the land when it was first locked down, who were living there with their families. In the coming months, all migrant labourers were encouraged by the government to leave and go back to their villages.

Since I was there, I said that we should keep the labourers on the premises, and that we would give their wages and food regardless of any work, because this would be a time when we could do the renovation without any guests or any outside interference.

They had open spaces to live, clean air, no pollution and they often caught fish from the river, with the occasional jungle fowl. The labourers were extremely happy to stay and we proceeded with the work. It was a difficult time because we were unable to get many supplies, as there were no trucks plying there between the cities of Rishikesh, Haridwar and Dehradun.

Work stopped at various times as construction material was not available. We came to a point where we had the labour but no construction materials and were unable to build. At that time, I thought the most sensible thing to do was to start the process of landscaping, which was a monumental task, and it was also something in which the labour could be usefully employed.

We actually reconstituted all the topsoil, removing truckloads of rock and barren undergrowth, and gradually levelled it. We also got organic manure from the local farmlands and finally it was ready for high-quality grass and exotic plants, flowers and scented creepers.

At this time, I realized that the building plans were not exactly what I had envisaged. I wanted to keep the outer facade of the current buildings and not really change their character. I also found that the landscaping plans had more concrete than I would have liked. So we went into an arrangement with the architects, where again we would use the expertise of their attention to detail, keep their supervisory staff at site with their strength, which was excellence in building. However, I kept the outer facade the same, had the insides completely gutted and restored and took on the landscaping of the property myself, which was more natural and organic.

Needless to say, I found books on landscaping, which I had picked up on my travels, never imagining how useful they would be one day! I always had a fetish for cookbooks and books on gardening, which I have collected on every trip I have been.

I used inspiration from these to create some surprisingly lovely garden and terrace areas. Later, when the project-management consultants and various agencies who were doing the work came up and saw the evolution of the land and asked who was doing it, we said we had a team of expert horticulturists. Actually, it was only me, the books and all my team, sworn to secrecy as to who was really the horticulturalist!

In June, when we started gradually getting some supplies, we were able to continue with the construction of the second block. The supplies were another story. Getting them up to Gular often meant that the trucks would need to be changed to smaller ones, everything cost twice the amount in freight and the lead times were erratic. Labour was difficult to get and at times trying to maintain the quality standards, which were paramount to the whole exercise, seemed virtually impossible! But we persevered steadily.

When we realized that the lockdown would not allow guests to visit before the end of the year, I spoke to the Neemrana management and said that we should actually get all the renovation done together since this was an unprecedented time, which we would never have otherwise got. They were not in agreement. These disagreements continued over months while the renovation was gradually being done, although the property was empty.

Finally, the main building had been kept closed for eight months and they did not want to hand it over to be redone. Without much choice, since it was the only building left while everything else was brand new, we just started work on it.

If that had actually happened earlier, we would have been able to get everything done much more smoothly and saved a lot of money and resources, but unfortunately it was not meant to be.

This was at a time when COVID tests were done every fifteen days. The labourers were constantly monitored by the police in the area and we were in a space where we were trying to do whatever we could, whenever we could.

Finally, by the time the place started coming together and a distinct difference could be felt, about ten months had passed. Those months cannot be repeated or done again because to redo an entire property in the time frame of a year, which is literally what happened, seems inconceivable. We had people cutting the marble, polishing the stone, putting in the tiles, ripping out the plumbing, entirely redoing the IT systems and waterproofing—it was unreal!

Everything was synchronized and happening simultaneously. My routine of the day would start at around six in the morning. I would come back to the house for lunch and then go back around four p.m., returning by about nine p.m., while the work often continued through the night. We had amazing teams of so many people who were committed to having this happen.

Of course, luckily I had Malathiji there who was also incarcerated with me for all these months, and every night after nine p.m. we would watch Pakistani dramas with bated breath!

We celebrated my father's life on his Barsi on 25 April 2020 as usual and a small team of skilled workers, who were to redo the temple for his Puja, worked round the clock to be able to complete the deadline. Finally, on the morning of the Puja, they had everything completed just in time.

It was just another sign, which had always happened through my life, that people whom I met on this journey made it possible for me to do certain things that otherwise seemed impossible.

No one subsequently could believe that this renovation, which happened between February and December 2020, could have changed the whole perception and appearance of what was The Glasshouse (the name of the hotel) metamorphosing into Anand Kashi, its original name, which means the Light of Inner Bliss.

———

In 2021, Sam and I were in the finalists' list for the twenty-second edition of the EY Entrepreneur of the Year Awards. It was a moment of great pride, and though it hasn't happened yet, I hope it is a forerunner of things to come.

Suddenly, we found that around the same time as last year, we were again in the midst of a second wave. Larger, more overwhelming than the last. The nightmare of last year revisited us with even more intensity. Although most Indians view catastrophes with a certain inevitability, this time there was a quiet rage amongst people.

In retrospect, the government had obviously declared victory over the virus too early despite, as we hear today, being aware of the possibility of a second wave.

We had never seen or envisaged a situation like this ever before. The disease spreading like wildfire amongst old and young—shortage of medicines, no hospital beds, no oxygen.

We were unable to have vaccination drives because there were no vaccines! There was no answer.

The most bizarre thing was allowing election rallies and religious congregations, which spiked the cases beyond control. More tragically, this time it had come closer to everyone, regardless of caste, creed, status or position.

Many people were true heroes who created WhatsApp groups and used Instagram to influence and make information accessible about available hospital beds, oxygen concentrators and much more. By August 2021, we finally started to see some normalcy with offices opening up, restaurants operating at full capacity, domestic travel thriving and smiles on everyone's faces, with the unending hope that the worst was behind them. Work from home was no longer feasible as it had been, and waking up in the morning and actually going to work became enjoyable again.

Unfortunately, this phase looked like it was meant to be short-lived, as rumours about a new variant came crawling in from the Western countries and the fear in India seeped in. The one positive thing this time was that majority of the people were vaccinated and this new variant, known as Omicron, while being extremely contagious, apparently had milder symptoms. The healthcare system was still intact. This was the silver lining as people continued to live their lives, wearing masks and accepting the fact that we will need to live with this flu.

Of course, tragedy has the effect of sometimes bringing out the best in people—acts of selflessness, philanthropy and even heroic behaviour from the most unlikely of us.

It is now the time to contain, prepare, reflect and get stronger for India.

And our place in the sun.

As I come to the end of this book, there is a sense of unfinished business being laid to rest.

It gives me great satisfaction to know that Anand Kashi has now come into its own. This unique legacy that my father could not enjoy, and I fought to retain, has now been built in his memory. It will allow generations of his family to experience this property's magical vibrations. When he passed away, I had promised myself that I would make that possible

We have just signed with the Taj Group of hotels, with whom we have had a long association, to open Anand Kashi as an exclusive Taj hotel in April 2022.

It is now finally in the right space.

44

Forest Essentials Today

Having never worked earlier in my life, I decided to start a company at forty-five, after my daughter got married and my responsibilities were not that apparent.

I did not even stop to think that I had no experience in manufacturing or retail. I did not know how to read a business plan, let alone put one together. I only had a very strong belief and determination to succeed, and refused to accept any setbacks, other than them being building blocks to where I wanted to go.

I am often told that I am a born entrepreneur, but when I look at myself, I find that all it really means is allowing yourself to learn things that you have not learnt before, and also to understand that many things you have learnt may not be the only way of doing things, and sometimes you need to unlearn.

In the course of my business, I have seen that many highly educated or experienced people bring a lot to the table, but sometimes also very dogmatic beliefs about the only right way to do things. I feel that this is a very narrow approach, because you don't let yourself be open to the fact that there may be other ways to get to a goal, rather than the only obvious ones.

The other fundamental edict I follow is that I always question when I am told that something is not possible to do. 'Why can't it be done?' The answer is either 'It's not possible' or 'Nobody does it like that' or 'There is no way it can be done as you suggest'. This has happened many times, both in my personal and professional life, and I have always found that when you want to find a way strongly enough, you can.

I am often asked about work–life balance. I think, perhaps, I had it easier because my children were grown-up when I started working, but I believe even if that had not been so, it is fine for work to sometimes be the priority, and sometimes your home to be the priority. I would not feel guilty either way, and I also don't think there is anything called a perfect work–life balance. As long as you can emotionally balance the two and feel good, that is what works. Lastly, I feel that when you start a business, and if it becomes successful, it is time to be level-headed and keep yourself grounded. Life is always a circle, and you never know when things go up or down. If you remain the same in both success and failure, only then are you truly successful.

I have no illusions that I can do any of this without my Forest Essentials family. I have been with them as much as I possibly could be, in any challenges both at work and in their personal lives that they bring to me.

When people are there for you without expectation, you stand with them as an extension of your own family.

Forest Essentials belongs to all of us. I know that I am driven by an expanding vision that I have for the company. I hope nothing can keep me from achieving the potential I see for it. I am grateful that the team is able to share my excitement, and that each time we endeavour to keep ahead of everyone else.

Today, we operate over 110 company-owned and company-run stores across twenty-eight cities in India, adding stores at a fairly rapid pace annually. Getting good locations was very difficult when we were starting out, as the brand was unknown and the proposed rentals extremely high. As we started getting popular, malls and high-street landlords began approaching us themselves, and it became slightly easier.

Another complicated issue we faced was that India is not one large homogenous country. It is more like a collection of small countries, each with its own language, food, God and culture, making it hard to build a brand that would appeal to everybody nationally. Not only every state but every city has its own nuances and we had to learn along the way and evolve as we expanded.

Our stores now average between five hundred to six hundred square feet and each and every one is in the top three performers in our segment, at both high streets and the malls that they are in. We have made sure they are always in a prominent location, refusing many stores along the way. That is another reason we have never shut down a store because of non-performance till date.

Besides our high-street and mall locations, we started to open, some years ago, stores in airports, or what is called Travel Retail. Traditionally, airports are extremely expensive with steep overheads and so very few brands manage to operate successfully and profitably. Given the versatility of our brand, we took the plunge and I am happy to now say that we have over fifteen airport stores across the country, both in metros and regional airports.

We also operate another sixty in-shop stores with our partners like Sephora and Nykaa. Running this entire collection of over 170 stores across the country requires a lot of patience, apart from infrastructure! Each landlord, mall developer and retailer comes with their own nuances and each and every one has to be handled carefully. It is all about maintaining a relationship with each one of them. Something actually done by Samrath very well!

Forest Essentials also has an institutional vertical, which caters to over 140 spas and three hundred hotels all over Southeast Asia. While the hotel business has never been profitable, it holds its head above water and is an important tool for creating awareness for the brand. Again, here it is all about relationships, exclusivity and creating personalized brand extensions. We have been working with some of our partners for well over ten years, something that is very unusual for this segment, given the number of players and brands that compete for this space.

Online, we distribute to over ninety-eight countries. We have our own website, which originally started in 2011 to cater to consumers who visited India but were unable to buy the products in their own countries. Today, it has an established presence and is growing rapidly month on month, and incidentally, we are the only Indian Ayurvedic brand in the luxury space, with the highest following on social media.

We also work with leading online channel partners, including Nykaa, Amazon and Myntra, where again we either lead in our verticals or are amongst the top three brands on their platforms. This despite never ever discounting the brand, which is the norm for online sales. It is a brief that we started with and have always refused to compromise on, which is sometimes difficult to keep to, but in the end, that is what defines the brand.

Our manufacturing facilities are spread over 100,000 square feet in Haridwar and Rishikesh in Uttarakhand and we still maintain our original workshop where we started. We have over 1,000 employees, many of whom have been with us over decades and still form an important part of our lives.

While we expanded nationally, it was important for us to create awareness on a national level, and in 2011–12, the only real medium was television. National television was prohibitively expensive and only large brands with limitless budgets could afford it. It was around that time that HD was starting to become popular and advertising more affordable. We decided to sponsor both *MasterChef Australia* and *Koffee with Karan*.

We had our first advertisement made by Wieden and Kennedy, an international agency with the Nike pedigree. Despite our initial reservations and the large costs involved, it was a resounding success and gave us national recognition beyond what we had envisaged.

Forest Essentials was finally poised to hit international markets, starting with the UK and then eventually the US, Asia and the Middle East, which was to happen in 2020 but was delayed because of the extraordinary circumstances of the pandemic.

We are the first Indian luxury brand to both represent the best of India as well as globally compete with the best brands in beauty, in keeping with our mission statement made two decades ago when we first started.

Over time, we have been patronized by royalty, film stars, industrialists and celebrities.

It is an honour that the Rashtrapati Bhavan has chosen to keep our products in its VVIP rooms. Many, including Presidents, Prime Ministers and First Ladies, have been gifted Forest Essentials products as part of Indian hospitality on their trip to India. Michelle Obama, Hillary Clinton and, more recently, Donald and Melania Trump also personally bought more of our products to give to friends and family back in the US.

The accolades that keep coming are humbling.

From 2011, I have had the surreal experience of finding myself in the top fifty list of Indian businesswomen in *Fortune* magazine! It's still there, much to the delight of my children and my Forest Essentials family. But for me, personally, I feel grateful that what I said to Mr Lauder about my vision for my company seems to have developed a life of its own.

Forest Essentials turns twenty-one years old this year. Ayurveda and beauty are an endless ocean of possibility. I want to create everything that is waiting to be discovered in that realm. Boundaries have to be constantly pushed and mistakes have to be learned from. The danger that comes with forging ahead in any sphere is that you continually have to reinvent yourself to remain in that position.

There are too many people who try and reproduce what you have done and are doing all the time.

I think one of the key reasons why we managed to stay ahead is that I am never satisfied. There is always more to do and the next time has to be better than the last. With that as a defining policy, the chances are a little better of retaining the position we have.

45

The Current Climate for Business

The government today has identified a promising road map for a progressive and supportive business environment, which includes the simplification of various procedures and subsequent red-tape reduction. This has been encouraging to businesses in general, particularly ours.

When I started out in 2000, the bureaucratic red tape and consequent corruption, even in just applying for the registration of an Ayurvedic formulation, was very daunting.

Our strong economic growth as the fifth-largest growing economy in the world is attributed to higher disposable incomes and a growing middle class, and includes increasing individual wealth and our large young population. The disposable income in the hands of the younger generation and the millennials' ability to spend has grown hugely over the last seven to eight years, which has been increasingly good for our business.

One case in point I would like to mention here is that this spending is not indiscriminate. Today, although the spending power is much higher, people, especially millennials, want to know the quality and origin of what they are buying, how it's made, the sustainability of the business, what are the benefits to them as well as how this impacts society at large.

The previously untapped rural sector and the lesser-developed tier-two and tier-three cities provide huge opportunities for growth, where health, fitness, nutrition, appearance, rest and mindfulness are now becoming top priorities. Forest Essentials had sensed this opportunity many years ago and already started booking stores in most of our smaller cities.

India has improved dramatically on its ease of doing business ranking in the last eight years and there is an intangible trust in its business environment.

The excellent highways and flyovers criss-crossing the entire length and breadth of our country bear testimony to our progressive development policies. I remember the drive from Delhi to Rishikesh in our early days, which would take eight to ten hours on dusty roads with potholes through towns and villages, with our car being stopped by a bullock cart or a tractor crossing the road. That was not that long ago.

Today it takes four and a half hours door-to-door from our home in Delhi to our home in Gular, which is an hour beyond the town of Rishikesh.

We are, I believe, poised to become the world's fastest-growing e-commerce market, driven by robust investment in the sector and rapid increase in the number of internet users. E-commerce is probably creating the largest revolution in the Indian retail industry and this trend is likely to continue in the years to come.

As a company, we have been extremely adaptive to the surge in e-commerce traffic and demand on our online platforms due to our already focused and growing digital competencies. This has fortunately held us in great stead.

Today, there is no longer a dichotomy between the online and offline retail industry, since the two are increasingly converging to maximize customer experiences. Experiential and seamless retail is now being seen as a 'point of touch' rather than just a 'point of sale'. This has been one of the strengths of Forest Essentials ever since its inception. As a brand, we focus on three aspects, which are customer education, customer experience and customer engagement. For us, beauty is more than skin deep, and our products are created to allow a moment of mindful relaxation, to enable inner serenity that reflects as outer radiance.

Most importantly, any customer who walks into our store or, for that matter, visits our website, is there for the personalized experience, trusted recommendations and value for products, which converts them into loyalists.

———

In this journey, I have often been asked what advice I would give to someone who wants to start a business. In the course of writing this book, I have thought about this in depth. I don't think I am really qualified to give advice on how to start a business, but if someone does ask, I can speak from my experience.

First, you have to love what you do. You must love it enough for it to be an overwhelming part of your life. You have to visualize it and live and breathe it.

Again, this is something I was told by my grandmother when I was a child. You can do anything you want but it must be the best it can be. If you want to be a cook, you must be the most skilled cook in the world; if you want to be a shoemaker you must make the best shoes in the world. It does not matter what you do, just how well you do it.

On a practical level, there is virtually no limit to how much you can spend in setting up a business. It is crucial to control costs with innovation and multitasking on many levels. In the end, if a business is not profitable, it does not justify it.

There is unfortunately no shortcut to hard work. This is a fundamental reality. Anything worth achieving requires a goal and then working towards it. Don't believe stories about the fact that some people are just so lucky—you define your path and opportunities come. If you keep waiting for the right moment, it may never come.

Finally, it is about never giving up. Never believing anyone who says that something is not possible. You can find a way and make anything happen.

You just have to want it enough.

46

Being Myself

At this present moment, I have come to a time in my life where I look at who I am, who I was and how destiny has shaped me. As a young girl, I should have been a lot more confident than I was, and in retrospect I had a lot to be confident about, but I never was. Very slowly over the years, I have created the complex fabric of who I am—the delicacy of the stitches, the varied hues of colour ranging from cool pastel washes to deep rich shades. The fabric is not uniform but has irregularities in its warp and weft. There are slashes in it in some places, which have been woven back—some invisible and some that can be seen.

I run my fingers over its smooth silken surface and I savour its feel, look and texture. I don't think I've ever taken the time to contemplate on myself ever, so it's an unusual occurrence for me when I'm asked to describe who I am, in parameters not defined by my work.

I do know that I love and am grateful for every facet of my life. I know each plant and each tree in both my homes, many of which have been planted and lovingly grown by me. Many are now lush, laden with luscious fruit or exquisitely scented flowers.

I have collected cookbooks for thirty years and have an amazing array overflowing in the kitchen, my bedroom and most of my living spaces. The preparation and cooking of varied cuisines from laboriously traditional to looking complicated but actually incredibly simple (I ask myself—is that it?) give me much joy.

My indulgences—there are many. I can't sleep without feather pillows, the softest lightest duvets, cashmere throws, pashmina blankets. My bedroom and bath always have a particular incense, which has a perfume as delicate as scented gossamer.

I love to write, and good stationery is something I find hard to resist. I collect beautiful notepaper and tissue-lined envelopes from Japan, richer matte paper from England and our own very fine handmade sheets.

I have been fortunate enough to travel for many years. The excitement of travel, exploring new cultures, experiencing things you haven't earlier, enjoying decadently stunning hotels and then looking forward to coming home is a ritual that is difficult to describe.

I have very eclectic choices when it comes to art, music, books, movies. I just know when I like something and, of course, being the person I am, I either love it or hate it! There has never been a middle road for me.

I also don't think that there is ever a time in my life that I have been bored. There is still a childlike curiosity about everything—making an intricate tapestry, painting a watercolour, using the mangoes in our orchard in season to make jams, pickles and juices, learning how to make a chicken coop (for my grandson) or creating a landscape from scratch. There is an endless list.

I am also very spiritual. I don't use the word religious because I really don't keep to conventional procedures of what should be done when. I treat God like a friend, to whom occasionally I say I'm sorry for doing something, and also thank Him for everything that He allows to happen every day.

I also believe that some things are meant to be, or preordained, and since there is nothing you can do to change that course, you must make the best of it.

In this retrospection, I look at my relationships with people. Again, if I love someone, there is nothing I would not do for them, regardless of who he or she is. Most of my friends are those who have been in my life for years, and strangely some have become precious not with time, but just the fact that they fit into your life in a way you can't understand.

I never forget a kindness, and a betrayal is forgiven but never forgotten.

I have learnt to appreciate unconditional love—someone who likes you the way you are, with your imperfections, and makes you feel good every time you see them.

I look at myself today, comfortable in my skin, able to say yes or no to things I don't wish to. I enjoy my independence as a woman as well as being feminine. One is not necessarily at the cost of the other. If I think of the choices I've made, I don't think I would change them, because each has contributed to the person I have become.

Too impulsive, emotional, determined, but still deeply compassionate and still vulnerable.

And yes, finally, I do like being who I am.

About the Author

Mira Kulkarni, Founder and Managing Director of Forest Essentials, is considered a far-sighted leader in the beauty industry for creating a revolutionary new segment in the market that did not exist earlier.

From handmade soaps to award-winning Indian Ayurvedic beauty products, nature-derived hair and skincare products have been a way of life for Kulkarni since childhood. Starting in 2000 and anticipating the need for enjoyable effective solutions in the skincare market, she has since curated a wide range of products, prepared according to ancient formulations with exacting standards, using fresh flowers, hand-pressed oils, medicinal roots, precious herbs and their infusions.

Kulkarni has been repeatedly honoured with several prestigious awards and commendations. She has been listed amongst Fortune India's Most Powerful Women in Business for ten consecutive years from 2011 to 2021. She has also been awarded the prestigious ETPrime Women Leadership Award for Businesswoman of the Year, 2019.

Papa

Mummy

With my mother at two

Me at eleven

Kamma Aunty and Jiti Mamu

With Jeetu at our reception

Samrath and Karishma, my son and daughter-in-law

Diviya and Hitesh, my daughter and son-in-law

A day spent with my granddaughter, Rhea, at seven

An evening with the boys, grandsons Shabad and Angad

My two granddaughters, Rhea and Samaira

With my friend, Guddu Nadar

With my childhood friend, Wanti Singh and Shiv Nadar

Rahul Bajaj—sharing bonds of friendship

Sam and I with the Chairman of
Estée Lauder, Leonard Lauder, at his home

At the Vogue Awards

Daniel Rachmanis, President,
Latin America at Estée Lauder, in Cannes

With my cousin, Vikram Singh

Adita and Sanjay Bhaskar

With my friend, Nina Gill

With my sister and brother-in-law, Anita
and Nechal Sandhu

Rekha Ganesan with the family on a visit
to Rishikesh

With my cousin, Nisha Singh

Bike ride with Hitesh

Sam and I

At Rishikesh with Sam, Karishma and Diviya

Hemant Achhra,
my sourcing companion

Mahesh Patel and his wife Usha—more
family than partners

Raju Kulkarni with the grandchildren

Sam with Neha Gadi, Head—
Institutional Sales (left), and
Jacqueline Tep Mishra, Head—
Retail Operations (right)

Sanjay Singh,
Head of Accounts

Heads of departments (L-R: Kartik Khanna, Sanjay Singh, Prakash Jha,
Marie Jonas, Suraj Dhillon, Manoj Singh, Jacqueline Tep Mishra,
Ira Kukrety, Arjun Singh)

Head Office team, Noida

2005

The original workshop at Lodsi

Tek Singh, my trusted man Friday

The original team in Lodsi: With Malathiji and Anuj in the front row;
standing extreme left: Diwan—our first key formulator

2022

The award-winning new facility at Lodsi

Awdhesh, Diwan and Vikram—here since the beginning

The Haridwar Factory team

Packaging with the original logo drawn by hand, 2002

The iconic Soundarya Range packaging, 2022

Our first store in Khan Market

Our store at Surat

Our Jodhpur store won the prestigious Architecture MasterPrize, 2022

Forest Essentials stores today